HUGH PALMER

Thames & Hudson

The Most Beautiful
Country Towns
of England

With 256 illustrations in color

Page 1
Totnes, Devonshire: Fore Street leads through the fifteenth-century East Gate, heavily restored in the early nineteenth century.

Title pages
Hastings, East Sussex: West Hill is a graceful sweep of urban downland above the centre of the Old Town.

Opposite
Bishop Percy's house, Bridgnorth, Shropshire.

First published in 2005 in hardcover in the United States of America by Thames & Hudson Inc., 500 Fifth Avenue, New York, New York 10110

thamesandhudsonusa.com

Library of Congress Catalog Card Number 2004195112

ISBN-13: 978-0-500-51235-7
ISBN-10: 0-500-51235-3

Printed and bound in Singapore by C. S. Graphics

Contents

Introduction

ENGLAND, not a huge country to start with, sometimes seems to be getting even smaller. Despite political initiatives designed to increase the power of local government, London's cultural dominance has been turning the whole country, some say, into one giant suburb. Modern communications have shrunk the place still further: new motorways have cut journey times between the major centres, and even the railway system, for long the butt of despairing jokes, is threatening to deliver an efficient alternative. As a result, visitors on a tight schedule can now 'do' England in a week. But how much they are missing! The true treasures, and the strongest bastions against the march of uniformity, lie off the beaten track, in England's country towns.

Their particular beauty is often a reflection of their rural setting, the very substance of the buildings expressing a connection with the surrounding land. The same local quarries may have, since the first beginnings, supplied the raw material: ruddy sandstone in Totnes, pale Bath stone for Bradford-on-Avon, and the rougher, warmer-toned variety of limestone for Chipping Campden in the Cotswolds. Further south on the Sussex Downs, there was nothing to be quarried but chalk, much too soft for building use. The houses here are of local brick, with local tiles hung to protect walls as well as roofs.

Generally, these towns have preserved enough of their original shape to make apparent the reason why they grew there in the first place. They might have sprung up, like Totnes or Stamford, at the most practical point for bridging or fording a river. The same river might also prove navigable, in an era when even sea-going ships, improbably miniature to modern eyes, could reach far up the Severn to Bridgnorth in Shropshire, or from the Wash down to Wisbech on the Cambridgeshire Fens.

A sheltered position on the coast might offer a safe haven for fishing-boats and trading ships. Unsheltered Hastings managed to do very well despite the failure of all attempts to build a harbour, remaining a seaport long after the other Cinque Ports, of which

Beverley's celebrated Minster dominates this view (opposite) *from the tower of St. Mary's parish church.*

7

A stout gate and a sleepy dog guard an elegant doorway in the close around St. Leonard's Church in Bridgnorth, Shropshire (above).

B uilt of local Bath stone at the height of the town's prosperity as a centre of the wool trade, Bradford-on-Avon's fine houses and The Swan Hotel rise up from the River Avon (opposite).

historic federation it was an original member, had lost their connection with the sea. Sometimes the establishment of a strategic fortress offered security, as at Alnwick or Ludlow, or great monasteries, like those of Shaftesbury and Bury St. Edmunds, could bring prosperity to local economies. The monks there often introduced innovative farming methods, as well as organizational skills, which made the best use of the surrounding farmland.

Whatever their various origins, the towns prospered where there were opportunities to make money. Buying and selling were the natural activities of the chief town of a district, to which local farmers brought their produce. Wool, grain and livestock were all carried, carted or driven in to the market-place, where bargains were made, money was banked, and supplies gathered. Thus did the towns become wealthy, steadily, and by accumulation, the merchants using their skills as the farmers did, to weather lean years as well as plentiful. Often the success of the place reached its pinnacle at the end of the eighteenth or the beginning of the nineteenth century. By that time, roads had improved enough for the country towns to become centres for a sizeable area. Easy access might dispose the owners of the country houses round about to build a stylish town house there. The apothecaries, lawyers, bankers and merchants built their mansions to match, and the town often became a social meeting-place where, during the 'season', a newly-built ballroom or assembly-room would witness the novel excitements of mixing between the increasingly permeable strata of society.

This was the age in which the centres of many of England's country towns became rich jewel-boxes of architectural delights. Few would quarrel with the notion that, after the Perpendicular style, their subtly proportioned Georgian houses are the greatest British contribution to architecture.

This prosperity, patiently won and by the nineteenth century well-established, typically insulated most of the country towns against the revolutionary changes of the Industrial Age that followed. Less

traditional places, in contrast, availed themselves of new capital, whereby factories, docks and railway stations would suddenly proliferate. In the well-founded country towns, however, even the arrival of the railway was often actively resisted, the local professional classes voted for the status quo, perhaps foreseeing the decline of the market-places in which their capital was invested. Stamford, a major staging post in the heyday of the stagecoach, saw nearby Peterborough balloon from obscurity after establishing its connection with the Great Eastern line. The huge expansion of Liverpool's docks eclipsed the previously important river port at Lancaster. But although the country towns often missed out on this transfusion of new wealth, they also escaped some of the worst excesses of expansion.

Towns that grew fat on the quickly made fortunes of manufacturing or of international trade were cut off from the surrounding countryside, as swathes of often mean housing sprawled outward, to accommodate the new urban labour force. Meanwhile, their centres were transformed by great bouts of civic spending, aimed at celebrating their new-found self-importance.

The quiet repose at best, or lean times at worst, experienced during this era by many of England's traditional country towns, have bequeathed to us many town centres still in their original size and scale. While in the past this made them vulnerable to the assault of motor car and heavy lorry, many of the towns have now been bypassed and, in part, turned back to pedestrian-only access. Small local shops and traditional markets thrive again, as local people tire of the bland uniformity offered by the out-of-town retail parks. The fortunate visitor can then while away a satisfying day, enjoying the harmony and proportion of ancient streets where the centuries have left behind them their intricate layers of history.

*E*pitome of the ancient country towns of England: Totnes, Devonshire, viewed from Kingsbridge Hill, presides over the River Dart on a summer morning (opposite).

A market in Bury St. Edmunds (above) has been held in the town since before the Norman Conquest. Moyses Hall, seen in the background, was built in the second half of the twelfth century.

The Northern Counties

Slate and stone in and near Ambleside (above and opposite): these local building materials make construction in the Lake District so distinctive. The town itself became a busy tourist attraction in the mid-nineteenth century, when the spread of the railways and improved roads encouraged people to explore the area, made specially seductive in the works of William Wordsworth.

THE CHALLENGE OF pacifying the English that faced the Norman conquerors, as it had the Romans before them, seemed all the more daunting the further north they looked. It was not just that the northern lands were so far away. The countryside is wild here, its hardy people raised, then as now, in a strong tradition of independence. For centuries, the already precarious livelihood of Northumberland's hill-farmers remained under constant threat from the lawless brigands of the Scottish Borders.

Even south of the Tyne in County Durham, it took great fortresses like that at Barnard Castle to keep the local nobility in order. Just over the Pennines, the wilds of Cumberland and Westmorland lay almost undiscovered until the idyllic beauty of their lakeland scenery captured the imagination of the Romantic poets. At the same time, a contrasting boom was happening just to the south, where the sudden expansion of Victorian industry inspired the building of great swathes of the urban north-east. Long before, the historic town of Lancaster was attracting trade from across the oceans, its tiny port on the River Lune watched over by its great castle.

Yorkshire, almost big enough to be a kingdom in its own right, has always cherished its independence. Its people are proud, but with the friendliness that comes of adversity shared. The moors and dales of the North Riding are now a much-loved National Park, but this has been an unforgiving terrain in times past. By contrast, the rich clay farmland to the south funded the building of the magnificent Beverley Minster for the monastery there.

Nowadays the north of England is bursting with energy, the slump following the collapse of its traditional industries thankfully consigned to the history books. Its wealth of natural beauty makes it a prime destination for visitors, and more permanent residents.

Alnwick

NORTHUMBERLAND

NORTHUMBERLAND IS A wild stretch of England. From the heather-topped Cheviot Hills, the great wide country rolls down to a majestic coastline. The county is large, but its population is relatively small and predominantly agricultural.

The town of Alnwick huddles cosily in the lee of its huge castle, which previously protected the town against the ravages of raiding parties from across the Scottish border to the north. Many of its older houses are built of the same local material – a storm-stained stone whose details are often blurred by the implacable effects of the sometimes bitter weather. Nevertheless, the town has a cheerful air, especially on Saturdays, when the colourful stalls of local produce enliven the newly restored, cobbled market-place. An equally welcome surprise is to be discovered inside the castle walls. Here, the ducal Percy family has lived without interruption since the castle was built. Now, the somewhat purposeful appearance of the castle has been considerably muted by the present Duchess's exuberant garden designs, which include a giant cascade and a recently opened tree-house complex worthy of Versailles.

Lured by such attractions, visitors arrive in increasing numbers. So does a new generation of incoming townsfolk, who are now swelling a once-dwindling population. To be at home in this incomparable countryside, with the city of Newcastle an easy thirty-mile journey away, is a welcome relief for many from the more populous parts of England.

F irst fortified in the fourteenth century, Alnwick Castle looms behind the sculpture of a straight-tailed lion, heraldic symbol of the Percy family (right). The lion stands on John Adam's Lion Bridge, spanning the River Alne, built in 1773 to replace an earlier structure destroyed in a flood.

*I*n the foreground to curving Narrowgate *(opposite)* stands one of the town's decorative water fountains, known locally as 'pants'. The western edge of Alnwick is graced by the fine Perpendicular tower of St. Michael's parish church *(right)*. *In the old market-place of the town a recently revived market lends colour to a background of weathered stone (below).*

*T*he impressive clock-tower of the 1771
town hall looms above elegant Fenkle Street
(above). *A place of fine public buildings, Alnwick
owes much of its architectural distinction to the
munificence of the Percy family (above right).
A more mundane sight is this archway leading to
the market-place (right), expressive of the gritty
quality of the local Northumbrian building.*

*F*inely proportioned Pottergate (above) *leads up to the Pottergate Tower, a structure in the 'Gothick' style of 1768 and once topped by a spire.*

*T*he valley of the River Alne (right) *unfolds below the magnificent terraces of Alnwick Castle.*

Ambleside CUMBERLAND

*T*he sandstone spire of St. Mary's church (above) cuts a distinctive form above the houses and inns of Ambleside. Until the collapse of the wool industry, the sound of the town's watermills (opposite) was so loud that the street next to the river was known as 'Rattle Ghyll'.

THE RESIDENTS OF Ambleside have mixed feelings, understandably, about the swarms of visitors who frequently outnumber them in their little town. Ironically, it was a local man who can take some of the credit (or the blame) for starting a tourist boom in the first place. William Wordsworth was born in nearby Cockermouth, and spent almost all of his life in the beloved Lakeland that was the inspiration of much of his prolific writing on the glories of nature.

But even before the visitors started to arrive, Ambleside was hardly a sleepy place. As well as providing a market for the local farmers, it was an early industrial centre, with the rushing fell-streams providing power for a number of small mills. From either of the two bridges over the main stream, Stock Beck, there is a good view of the remaining mill, last used for spinning wool. The present Bridge Street was even known as 'Rattle Ghyll', from the clanking of all the water-

wheels. Now the trudge of stout boots indicates the town's main activity: catering for and accommodating the thousands who head for the hills each year.

Wordsworth was ambivalent about the tourists of his day, too, impatient even with the admirers who used to queue at his gate hoping for an audience. As for the idea of sharing the Lakes with thousands of holidaying Lancashire mill-workers, he proved himself a staunch élitist. In his seventies he composed a 'Sonnet On The Projected Kendal and Windermere Railway' : 'Is then no nook of English ground secure from rash assault?'.

That battle he lost, but his passion inspired successive generations of conservationists, and happily the majestic scale of the hills themselves still allows anyone who sets out for a day's walk from Ambleside a fair chance of wandering alone in the footsteps of the poet himself.

*A*mbleside is a place of sturdy buildings and solidly built stone walls (opposite, above and below left). *The High Street* (above), however, does reflect the prosperity brought by the thousands of visitors to the dramatically picturesque countryside around (overleaf).

Barnard Castle CO. DURHAM

T he improbably French-looking Bowes Museum (above), designed by Jules Pellechet and begun in 1869, houses important collections of furniture, ceramics and Spanish art, originally acquired by John Bowes, son of the tenth Earl of Strathmore, and his actress wife, Josephine Benoîte. The ruins of the castle which gave the town its name are another important focal point (opposite); they dominate the two-arched bridge across the River Tees.

FOR CENTURIES, the *raison d'être* of this town was its great castle – first built above the rushing river Tees by the Norman baron, Bernard de Bailleul. From this stronghold, he sought to control the constantly rebellious northern noblemen. Fighting came to the castle itself during Elizabeth's reign, when a rebel Catholic force laid siege to it. Damage to the fabric was slight, at least compared to that wrought later by the Vane family, who purchased the castle as a source of spare parts for their own seat, nearby Raby Castle. The local people were not slow to follow this lead, and the castle was gradually dismantled as the town grew.

Many of the fine houses that line the main streets are built from the pilfered stone, insouciantly turning their backs on the ruins that once gave the town its name. The main road in from the east, having become the broad and handsome Galgate, turns abruptly left to skirt the castle. Here an even prouder sight presents itself – a gently curving sweep of wide cobbled market-place, which terminates at the octagonal Market Cross, just before a steep hill, The Bank, which runs down towards the river. The Cross is a fine and characterful building, with plenty of room for the town's youth to take their ease where their great-grandmothers used to sell eggs and butter in the shade of the portico.

From here, the road out of town passes by another monumental building which, like the castle, is discreetly tucked away. Glancing through a gateway, the passing visitor may wonder at an extraordinary sight: a French-style château, seemingly transported directly from the Loire valley. In fact, this is the wonderful Bowes Museum, a legacy to his native Teesdale of the Victorian worthy John Bowes.

*S*ome of the town's finest buildings line The Bank (above), which leads
downhill from the Market Cross to the Tees. St. Mary's parish church
(opposite above), *mainly Norman but with a nineteenth-century tower, looks
down over Barnard Castle's houses, many of them notable for elegant detailing*
(opposite below).

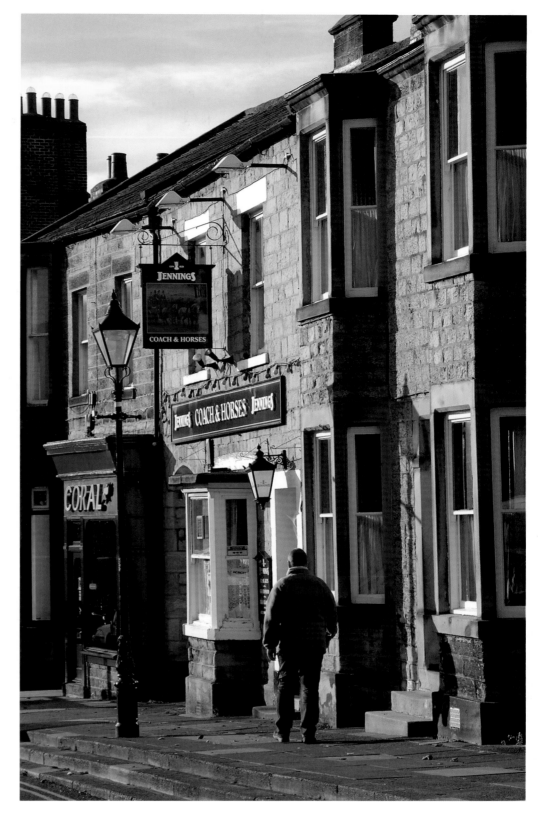

*T*he eighteenth-century Market Cross (opposite), *distinguished by its Tuscan arcade, was given to the town in 1747, since when it has been used variously as a court-house, gaol, town hall and butter market. The Bank and Galgate, the two main streets, can furnish the visitor with a variety of merchandise* (this page).

Beverley YORKSHIRE

P re-eminent among the architectural treasures of Beverley are the Market Cross, dating from 1714, and St. Mary's church, with its tower of 1524 (above). Its most splendid building, however, is undoubtedly the Minster, whose monumental north porch can be seen here soaring above Highgate (opposite).

THAT ENTHUSIAST OF England's hidden architectural treasures, John Betjeman, aptly described Beverley as, 'A place made for walking and living in'. He would probably have elected to enter the town on foot through its remaining medieval gate, North Bar, which gives on to the cobbled North Bar Within and, a short walk past the parish church of St. Mary's, to the spacious market-place. Here, under the resplendent Queen Anne embellishments of the Market Cross, a lively market is held every Saturday. The rest of the week, inevitably, the area is jammed with parked cars, whose owners are busy patronizing the shops and pubs of the town centre. The main shopping street, however, has been made a precinct for pedestrians; it follows a winding route to the small square whose name, Wednesday Market, denotes another weekly tradition, recently revived. These narrow streets, still bearing their evocative names, Toll Gavel and Butcher Row,

are largely unchanged, in both scale and appearance. A former chemist's shop, at 44 Toll Gavel, has a pair of carved snakes twisting round the columns of its doorway, symbols of Aesculapius, Greek god of medicine. More spacious by far is the area on the eastern edges of the town, where the heavenly Minster rears up to a majestic height from the tranquil setting of its grassy precincts.

This area of Yorkshire, tucked in just north of the giant river Humber, is pleasantly unfrequented, in contrast to the spectacular and much-visited dales and moors lying to the north. Beverley itself, looking like a miniature and unspoilt version of York, is content with quiet pre-eminence over its own less fashionable corner of the county. The land around is flat (providing an ideal site for the town's celebrated racecourse, just off the York Road), while the Minster's twin Gothic towers can be seen for many miles around, a proud landmark.

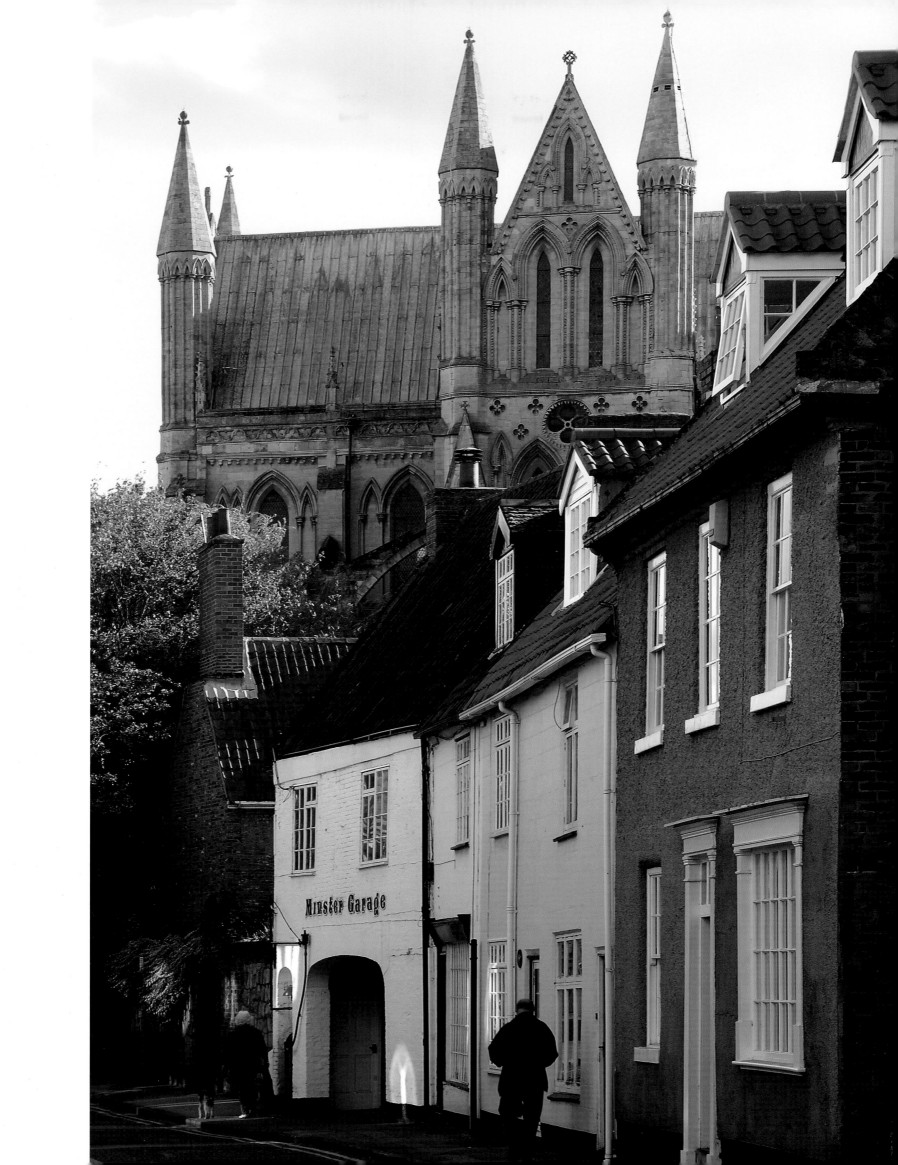

*T*he town is remarkable for the number of original
façades and features retained by its houses and
commercial premises (right *and* opposite). *Just inside
the one remaining medieval gate, North Bar, a neat row
of town houses is still graced by its original forged iron
step railings (above). A more boisterous note in this
sedate and elegant place is struck by this colourful
figurehead adorning the front of one of Beverley's inns
(above right *and* opposite).*

*T*he Georgian houses around the Minster
(below) *make a perfect foil to the majestic*
Gothic of its soaring west towers (opposite).

*C*onsidered to be one of the most beautiful parish churches in England, St. Mary's has architectural features dating from the twelfth century to the time of the Reformation (opposite). The splendour of its nave (right) is an emphatic reminder of the importance of this church, once the centre for the Guild of Minstrels in the north of England.

Lancaster LANCASHIRE

HIGH ABOVE THE River Lune, Lancaster's massive castle still dominates the town. It dwarfs the priory church of St. Mary's, with which it shares an elegant hill-top precinct, a place of stone-paved streets, lawns, trees and quiet rows of fine Georgian houses – all the accoutrements of a cathedral close, in fact. It comes as something of a surprise to find that the formidable gatehouse is still guardian to a functioning prison and court-house inside the castle walls.

Along St. George's Quay, pleasantly restored warehouses and workshops are reminders of Lancaster's early prosperity. The docks are on a tiny scale, and it is hard to imagine that the town was once the fourth port in England. This was in the early days of the West Indies trade, when slave ships came back with ballast of mahogany, before the sugar plantations were fully established. As a result, local furniture-makers, the famous firm of Gillow among them, became pre-eminent in the creation of the opulent designs of British High Victorian décor.

Lancaster's shipping activities were eventually eclipsed by the development of the docks at Liverpool; but by that time the town was enjoying a second great boom. This was largely inspired by the manufacture of that revolutionary floor covering, linoleum, pioneered by the local oilcloth makers, Williamson & Son. They dominated the world market for almost a century. James Williamson the younger, born in 1842, was the archetype of a Victorian paternalistic businessman. Not a believer in the necessity for shareholders, or even business partners, he ran the company single-handed until his death in 1930. He was a legendary, as well as astute, public benefactor, though any outlay usually commanded a healthy return. Rising from the office of mayor to become the town's Member of Parliament, he ended up as Lord Ashton, one of the first 'industrial peers'. Impossible-to-miss reminders of his largesse include the colossal town hall, looking over Dalton Square, and, on top of Williamson Park, which already rises almost five hundred feet above the town, a huge domed confection rising another hundred and fifty feet: the Ashton Memorial.

*O*n *an already high hill above Lancaster, the Ashton Memorial reaches even higher* (right). *Begun in 1906, this folly was built by the local linoleum and oilcloth magnate, Lord Ashton, in memory of his wife. It is now a concert venue.*

*T*he streets of Lancaster are graced with a wealth of impressive monuments and buildings, including a statue of Queen Victoria (above), erected at the behest of Lord Ashton in 1907, and the façades along Market Street (above right). Lancaster Castle, or John of Gaunt's Castle as it is often called (right), shares its mound high above the River Lune with Lancaster Priory and St. Mary's church.

The Midland Counties

*B*y association the cultural jewel of the Midlands, Stratford-upon-Avon, Warwickshire, also has a wealth of old houses and inns decorated with fine carving (above). Another kind of gem is set in warm Cotswold stone in Chipping Campden, Gloucestershire (opposite).

IN THE HEART of England can be found the quintessence of the shires of popular parlance: rich farmland in gently undulating countryside. Much of the region, however, was once covered by forest. From here, traditionally, came the raw material for the English Navy, the 'Wall of Oak' that famously confounded the ambitions of Philip of Spain. This tree, noted for its strength and elasticity, was also ideally suited to building use, resulting in the many fine timbered houses that have weathered the centuries to grace country towns of the Midlands to the present day.

Not all of the Midland counties were forested: the wilder expanses of Derbyshire's Peak District have been treeless since the Ice Age. In a sheltered vale nearby, however, sits the spa town of Buxton, its majestic public buildings made from the local limestone, its inhabitants benefiting from the healthy air and famously pure water. Also exposed are the rolling hills of the border country with Wales, the Marches. Here, the town of Ludlow first owed its importance to its castle, built to keep an eye on unruly neighbours to the west. Only after the campaigns of Edward I were these lands able to prosper from the rich potential of their pastures and orchards.

To the north, the great River Severn runs across the county of Shropshire. It once brought a flourishing trade far inland to Bridgnorth. The fine church of St. Mary's is built of red Triassic sandstone – and in its long course, the river lays bare a variety of local stone, in many colours and textures. By the seventeenth century, as elsewhere in the country, the fashion for brick had taken over. Not so in the Cotswolds, however, where the honey-coloured limestone was always the material of choice. The gentle hills that supplied it were also ideal for sheep, and by the late Middle Ages the resplendent 'wool towns', such as Chipping Campden, rivalled those of the eastern counties in prosperity.

Loveliest of all the shires is surely Warwickshire, at least the part of it that has escaped inclusion into the giant conurbation around Birmingham. At Stratford, lapped by the matchless perfection of the River Avon, one feels truly at the heart of England, near its spiritual heart too – the birthplace of the country's incomparable Bard, William Shakespeare.

Bridgnorth
SHROPSHIRE

THE STYLISH WAY to arrive in Bridgnorth, and most in keeping with the area's industrial heritage, must undoubtedly be by train. The busy line from Kidderminster once served stations further north whose names are potent reminders of the early stages of the Industrial Revolution: Coalport and Ironbridge. Once closed, it has now been re-opened as far as Bridgnorth by the enthusiastic volunteers of the Severn Valley Railway, who steam up and down in lovingly preserved locomotives saved from the scrap-heap.

The town's commercial importance goes far back before the arrival of the railway in 1862, however. It was an important port on the Severn, which by the seventeenth century was the busiest river in England after the Thames. Goods travelling to and from the great seaport of Bristol would be piled on the quayside beside the bridge, once overlooked by large warehouses. In those days, the only way to the upper part of the town, one hundred feet above, was by pack-horse. The ancient Cartway still weaves its way up there, between a picturesque jumble of ancient houses and cave-dwellings. Many of the houses have stout shutters at street-level, to protect their windows from swaying pack-horse loads.

Emerging breathless in High Town, the visitor will see the bustling High Street, broadening to accommodate the town hall of 1652, past whose pillared base the traffic weaves. At the other end are the remains of the castle, mostly destroyed in the Civil War, and one of the town's two principal churches, the late-Georgian St. Mary's, designed by Thomas Telford. From here, a promenade offers fine views along the river valley and a bird's-eye view of Low Town beneath. A pleasant stroll leads to another thoughtful Victorian amenity, an exasperating discovery for the visitor who, in ignorance, has tackled the challenging ascent on foot – one of England's few cliff railways.

Half-timbering in Bridgnorth: the town hall (above) *sits in the middle of the busy High Street, while Bishop Percy's house* (opposite) *is surrounded by the venerable dwellings ranged up the sandstone cliffs rising from the River Severn. The house, one of the few to survive a fire in 1646, takes its name from the Rev. Dr. Percy, Bishop of Dromore, who was born there in 1729.*

*T*he streets of Bridgnorth are full of pleasant domestic architecture *(below)*, *as well as grander ecclesiastical edifices, such as the church of St. Mary Magdalene* (right), *designed by Thomas Telford, or that of St. Leonard's, a largely Victorian restoration of a very ancient edifice* (far right).

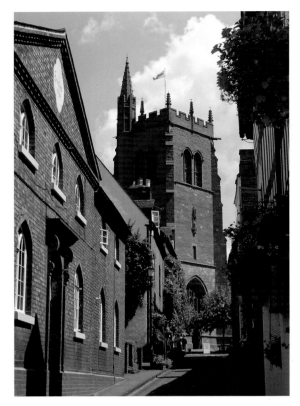

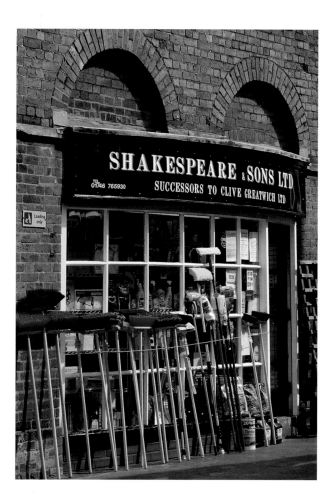

*I*n Listley Street is just one of many intriguing shop
frontages in Bridgnorth (above left). *The town's position
on a steep incline above the River Severn is reflected in its
division into High Town and Low Town, the two connected
by England's oldest – and inland, the steepest – surviving cliff
railway, which has been in operation since 1892* (left). *In
the busy High Street there is more half-timbering, viewed
here from the town hall* (above).

*T*he various levels of Bridgnorth
make it a place of delightful,
private corners (left), which can
suddenly yield up magnificent vistas,
like this view down to the River
Severn (opposite).

Buxton DERBYSHIRE

In the 1780s the fifth Duke of Devonshire commissioned York architect John Carr to design Buxton's famous Crescent (above), part of a plan to promote the town as an important spa. Part of the complex later became the Devonshire Royal Hospital, to which a huge dome was added in 1880 (opposite).

THE FAMOUS BUXTON water makes a long and slow progress through the limestone area of Derbyshire's Peak District, before it emerges, energized and purified, in the 'Spa Town in the Hills'. The Romans, those connoisseurs of thermal bathing, were keen on their rest cures taken in Aquae Arnemetiae, as they named the town. Ever since, there has been a steady flow of visitors attracted by the health-giving properties of the water, as well as the clean air of the Peak District. The fifth Duke of Devonshire (whose family's great palace at Chatsworth lies only twelve miles away) decided to capitalize on the spa boom of the late eighteenth century and develop the market town into a fashionable resort. Many of the charming public buildings that grace Buxton date from that period, including the elegant Crescent, reminiscent of its Royal counterpart in Bath.

The town was laid out so that the green spaces, which extend liberally into the town centre, give a true sense of 'rus in urbe', especially in the

Pavilion Gardens, laid out by Edward Milner, a pupil, appropriately, of the Devonshires' favourite, Joseph Paxton. The architect of London's Crystal Palace would also have approved of Milner's giant conservatory, the Winter Gardens, offering year-round climatic relief when the weather reminds the visitor just how far north Derbyshire actually lies.

The English picked up the curious habit of buying drinking water in bottles from their holidays in France, so perhaps it was fitting that Buxton Water should end up in the hands of the French giant, Perrier. The new proprietors got off on the wrong foot with the townsfolk, however, when they made moves to shut off the much-patronized public fountain of St. Anne's Well, just in front of The Crescent. In the end the company took the diplomatic option, perhaps considering themselves not well placed to complain about people impudent enough to help themselves to what comes naturally out of the ground.

*B*uxton's Pavilion Gardens (opposite) *would bring distinction to any capital city. The Pavilion itself (above)* was *originally built in 1871, then extended in 1875 to incorporate an iron and glass concert hall. In addition to the vistas of its green spaces, Buxton is also a place of pleasant detail: impressive town houses* (left), *and the famous St. Anne's Well* (far left), *from which townsfolk can still draw the renowned water.*

The Midland Counties · 57

*B*uxton's exquisite Opera House (above) *dates from the town's Edwardian heyday as a fashionable spa. The work of Frank Matcham, the most successful theatre architect of his time, it opened its doors in 1903; fittingly, it now stages a hugely popular annual festival of the works of Gilbert and Sullivan. The town is still bustling and energetic* (right), *but the visible presence of the moors around, the greenery of the area known as the Slopes, laid out in 1818, and the Pavilion Gardens* (overleaf) *provide a welcome contrast to the stone terraces of the centre.*

Chipping Campden GLOUCESTERSHIRE

The seventeenth-century silk trader and civic benefactor, Sir Baptist Hicks, left a very distinctive architectural imprint on the town, in the form of twelve almshouses (opposite) *and the Market Hall* (above). *The church dedicated to St. James – looming high above the almshouses – contains monuments in memory of Hicks.*

OF ALL THE famous 'wool towns' of the Cotswolds, Chipping Campden is probably the finest. It is certainly the best preserved: a lasting high-tide mark of the extraordinary wealth that the wool trade brought to the region. The perfection of the High Street, with its curving, uninterrupted sweep of honey-coloured houses, has entered the popular imagination so pervasively, by means of so many tin trays, calendars and chocolate boxes that it appears almost as a vision out of some pleasant fantasy of a bygone age. Ancient inns, with their hanging wooden signs, seem to be waiting for a coach and team of horses to clatter in. Instead, there is the smooth hiss of the air-conditioned tour buses as they disgorge the summer crowds, eager to rifle the antique shops for some fragment to take back, like a talisman, to the real world.

The charming Market Hall, midway down the street, almost shared the same fate as more portable antiques. There were plans (happily abandoned at the outbreak of World War II) for it to be dismantled and re-erected in the United States. It was built for the 'womenfolk of the Town' by one of Chipping Campden's great benefactors, Sir Baptist Hicks, later the first Lord Campden. He also built the lovely row of almshouses, all still in use, that runs up to the church. Behind the stone wall opposite, he also built for himself a magnificent house, of which one can see only the tantalizing remains. All the rest was destroyed by fire during the Civil War. Not, according to legend, as a result of enemy action; Sir Baptist, a passionate Royalist, preferred to set it alight rather than have it fall into the hands of Cromwell's Parliamentarians.

*M*any of the houses of the town – especially those built by wool merchants between the fourteenth and seventeenth centuries – are constructed from the warm Cotswold stone, which gives the whole place its characteristic honey colour (above). Some contrast is provided by the half-timbering of such buildings as this sixteenth-century former inn (opposite).

*T*here is a peculiar kind of perfection about the detailing of the
streets of Chipping Campden: on the High Street (opposite);
on Sheep Street (above left); on Westington Hill (above right).

*T*he town lies snugly beneath Westington Hill, which yields this magnificent view from the south-west. It inspired one 1930s writer to comment, 'Those who believe in love at first sight should view Chipping Campden from Westington Hill'.

*O*nce described by John Betjeman as 'the most
perfect town in England', Ludlow's delightful
streets (above) are dominated by the massive tower of St.
Lawrence's church (opposite), the largest in Shropshire.
Here it is seen looming above the splendid overhanging
gables and decorative barge-boards of Broad Street.

Ludlow
SHROPSHIRE

WALLED TOWNS ARE a common enough
phenomenon in France, ideally in
combination with an unscalable hill; lack
of such protection would have spelt disaster
during the centuries when marauding armies
were a constant threat. England, through a
combination of naval supremacy and good
luck, has been free from the attention of
invaders for almost a thousand years, at least
from the south; Hadrian's Wall has often
proved a less reliable barrier than the English
Channel. Hence, her walled towns are
relatively few in number; and Ludlow is
perhaps the finest of them.

It lies in the heart of the border country
with Wales, the so-called Marches, and
played a central role in keeping order over
this often disputed hilly countryside. As well
as its mighty castle, which sits inside the walls
and shares the town's defences, it has, for
good measure, a hill site and a protective,
encircling river, the Teme.

Of the original walls much still stands,
although only one of the seven original
gateways survives, at the foot of Broad Street.
The gateways did more than keep the town
safe; they also helped to control entry,
keeping out undesirables as well as making it
practical to extract dues from traders using
the busy market. The walls also preserved the
town from that more insidious enemy – slow
destruction by careless development.

Essentially, the medieval plan of Ludlow's
streets is still intact. A grid is formed by the
three main streets, which contain a wealth of
Georgian houses (Ludlow boasts no fewer
than five hundred listed buildings), and then
there is the extensive Market Place, which
abuts on to a charming warren of alleys
spreading out from the Butter Cross. Also
preserved is the amazing skill of local
carpenters, visible on the half-timbered
frontages of the oldest buildings, which date
back to the seventeenth century.

*L*udlow's medieval street plan remains intact, although the streets are mainly lined with Georgian frontages (above *and* right). *The presence of earlier timbered buildings* (opposite), *however, emphasizes the antiquity of the place.*

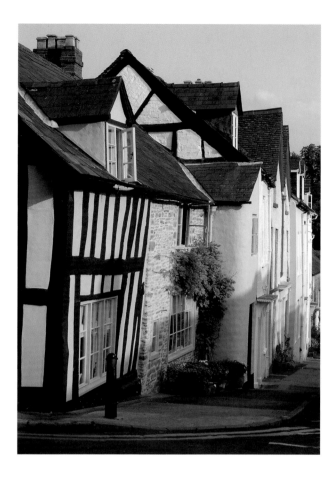

E *very part of the town yields fresh and fascinating*
perspectives. The castle, high above the River
Teme (opposite), *has Norman, medieval and Tudor*
features. Mill Street (above left) *has some fine timber*
construction; a quiet corner offers a glimpse of the pink
sandstone porch of St. Lawrence's (left), *while another*
viewpoint reveals the hills of Shropshire (above), *so*
famously celebrated by A. E. Housman.

Stratford-upon-Avon
WARWICKSHIRE

STRATFORD WOULD STILL be a charming place to visit, even if its most famous son had been born elsewhere. An otherwise unassuming but utterly charming market town, it sits compactly beside a perfect stretch of that loveliest of England's rivers, the Avon. The countryside around is still richly rural, despite the presence of the huge conurbation of Birmingham not far to the north. Although the weekly market, established in the twelfth century, still functions strongly, it is the influx of pilgrims that now supports the town. The attraction of genius draws them from all corners of the globe, following a trail whose first indications are easy enough to pick up from the signs announcing the county of Warwickshire as 'Shakespeare Country'.

An enjoyable stroll round the town takes in the well-preserved houses connected with the playwright: his father's house in Henley Street, his wife's cottage in Shottery and, most impressively, his daughter Susanna's house, Hall Croft. They all provide a fascinating glimpse into how life was lived in Elizabethan times, but the Bard himself, appropriately, remains a shadowy presence. The chief treasure should be the imposing house, New Place, that he bought for his retirement, after the arduous ups and downs as 'Fortune's knave' in London. Unfortunately, all that remains at the corner of Chapel Street and Chapel Lane is an empty plot, albeit decorated with a period knot-garden. The house itself was pulled down by a subsequent owner, the Reverend Francis Gastrell, after a feud with the town authorities. He had earlier made himself unpopular by chopping down Shakespeare's favourite mulberry tree, exasperated by the unending stream of devotees. Present-day visitors are more fortunate – one minute's walk from here to the river will take them to the box-office of the Royal Shakespeare Company's theatre.

Dating from the time of Shakespeare, The Falcon Hotel presents a delightful timbered façade along Chapel Street (above). And it was in 1564 that Shakespeare was christened in Holy Trinity church (opposite), where the original font still stands. There is a monument to the Bard – buried here – on the north wall of the chancel.

*T*he Guild Chapel, close to
The Falcon Hotel (left), *was
originally built in 1269 for a group
of influential citizens known as the
Guild of the Holy Cross. It was
almost entirely rebuilt in the
fifteenth century by Hugh Clopton,
a Guild member who became Lord
Mayor of London.*

*T*he stone bridge over the Avon (left), *known simply as Clopton Bridge, is another memorial to Stratford's great benefactor. A more modern signature sight on the Avon is the distinctive 1930s form of the Royal Shakespeare Company's theatre (above), designed by Elizabeth Scott.*

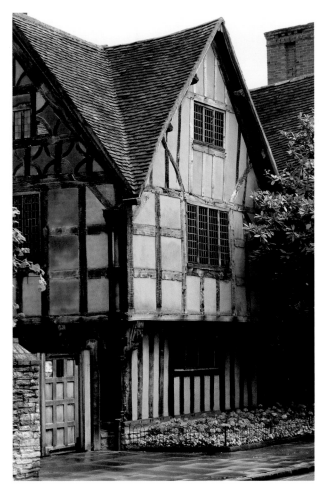

*V*arieties of timberwork in Stratford: the town has some *fine Victorian examples* (above right), *as well as the more traditional forms of the home of Shakespeare's daughter, Susanna* (right). *A particularly fine period building is Harvard House* (above), *birthplace of John Harvard, founder of the famous university, and now home to the Museum of British Pewter. It was built in 1596 by Alderman Thomas Rogers, a butcher, whose trade is denoted by the carving of a bull's head on the façade.*

Stratford's medieval architectural heritage is rich indeed: an early timbered house near the market-place (below); the Guildhall (right) of 1269.

The Eastern Counties

The rich architectural heritage from all periods enjoyed by the country towns of the east of England reflects their times of great prosperity: an elegant Georgian doorway (above) in Bury St. Edmunds, Suffolk; the double hammer-beam ceiling (opposite) of the fifteenth-century church of St. Peter and St. Paul, Swaffham, Norfolk.

THE EASTERN COUNTIES often seem to be out on a limb, although a first glance at a map of England would suggest otherwise. They are close to the capital, their low-lying terrain offers no natural barriers, and the gentle bulge described by East Anglia's coast has none of the dramatic extremes of, say, the West Country. Invaders were certainly attracted by the arable possibilities of the region; its climate is drier and warmer, and its soil lighter than other parts of England. It benefited from inclusion in the prosperous Roman civil zone; later, it spent several centuries under Danish control.

These counties were at the centre of English life in medieval times, when the production of wool and the small-scale weaving of cloth made the region famously prosperous. From Lincolnshire to Essex, the country towns became showcases for rich building. Materials varied. Stamford in Lincolnshire was built almost entirely from the local limestone. Further south, although large-scale brick production did not take off until the sixteenth century, the absence of stone and the abundance of clay encouraged the development of a distinct building style. Oak trees thrive on a clay soil; thus, the skills of building carpentry achieved their finest expression in the timbered structures and decorative woodwork of the Suffolk and Essex towns.

Their churches, too, rightly hold pride of place in England's architectural treasury. The Gothic style reached its apogee in the fifteenth century, with the great flowering of the Perpendicular. Many a modest church was lavishly rebuilt by the wool merchants and their guilds, creating monuments to piety in the form of soaring towers, visible for scores of miles over the low-lying landscape.

The countryside they still dominate is thinly populated, despite the creep of urban sprawl that affects the areas nearest the capital. Norfolk in particular, with its fine understated and undervisited north-facing coastline, offers a tranquillity unmatched elsewhere in southern England, and Lincolnshire, richly endowed with testaments to its medieval greatness, remains surprisingly remote.

Bury St. Edmunds   SUFFOLK

*M*uch of Bury's discreet elegance is derived from its wealth of seventeenth- and eighteenth-century buildings and detailing. Thus, a fanciful Georgian decoration (above) surmounts a porch near Westgate Street. Cupola House (opposite), built in 1693, is considered to be one of the finest of the town.

'THE NICEST TOWN in the world', William Cobbett declared of Bury St. Edmunds. His judgement still holds good today. It is partly Bury's very antiquity that makes it such a friendly place: the main streets, laid out many centuries ago, have an intimate scale that is instantly welcoming. When the Normans arrived there, they found a monastery that had already been in existence for four hundred years. It had steadily grown in importance, particularly since acquiring the remains of a Saxon King, Edmund, who had met a martyr's end at the hands of an earlier band of invaders, the Danes. The Normans' appointee, Abbot Baldwin, greatly expanded the monastery and, with it, the town.

Although the monks were responsible for stimulating much of Bury's growing prosperity – they certainly began the tradition of brewing the delicious local beer – the townsfolk cannot have been entirely happy with the monastery's control of matters political and economic. After the death of Edward II, during the wave of unrest that then swept the country, they broke into the monastery

and sacked it. A purposeful fortified gate was erected shortly afterwards (built by local people as a penance), but the monastery did not survive the general dissolution during the Reformation. The gatehouse still stands, massive and beautiful, guarding the precincts, but the visitor passing through it will find no more than some stumps of masonry, dotted around a spacious park, in which the pillagers' descendants can enjoy their tranquil walks and picnics.

This gate looms over Angel Hill, the elegant slope that divides the abbey grounds from a network of little streets, lined with many original Georgian shop-fronts. There are many pleasing echoes of this collision of scales: the huge Greene King brewery on Westgate Street faces the tiny Theatre Royal; two little rivers, the Lark and the Linnet run along in the shadow of the imposing cathedral church of St. James; next to the market-place, Robert Adam's exquisitely grand Market Hall is just round the corner from a most congenial point of pilgrimage: officially the Smallest Pub in England, ' The Nutshell'.

*R*eminders of the town's importance in medieval times stand out amid the ordered façades of Georgian Bury (opposite *and* right); *to the left of the 1804 front of the Athenaeum rises the Norman gate-tower* (above).

A town with a brewing tradition, exemplified in the Greene King Brewery *in Westgate Street* (above right), *Bury also boasts what is reputedly the smallest pub in the land* (above left), *aptly named 'The Nutshell'. Another little gem in the town is the Theatre Royal* (opposite), *which opened its doors in 1819.*

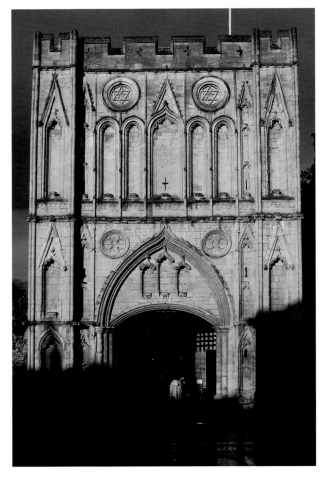

*T*reasures of medieval Bury: the interior of St. Mary's church (above) *is famous for its hammer-beam ceiling, dating from the early fifteenth century; the gatehouse to the abbey grounds* (above right *and* right) *was destroyed by the townsfolk in the riots of 1327, then later rebuilt by them.*

Quiet corners of the town: peace and tranquillity reign in the churchyard of St. Mary's (above); the window of a tiny town house (right) is enlivened with decorations for Easter.

Saffron Walden

ESSEX

SAFFRON WALDEN NESTLES cosily among
the wooded hills of northern Essex, where the
grand spire of St. Mary's stands out as a proud
landmark. This is claimed to be the largest parish
church in the county, and it is certainly the most
lavish. By the time of its construction, the town
had benefited from the wool boom that enriched
its neighbours to the north in Suffolk. The rest of
the town is older, and there is an intimate charm
about the streets of its centre, whose layout has
not changed since medieval times.

There is no feeling of claustrophobia here,
however. The great majority of the houses, inns
and shops that line the streets are little changed
from their originals, so all is pleasantly in
proportion. This makes the town a delight to
explore, to admire not only the quaint shapes of
the overhanging gables, but also the decorative
plasterwork peculiar to the region: pargeting. In
the centre, Market Square offers more space for
such flamboyant oddities as the Italianate Corn
Exchange, dating from 1848. Near at hand is
the town's Common, formerly Castle Green,
on which there is record of a Royal Tournament
being held in 1252. Nowadays, these fourteen
acres of green space are criss-crossed by citizens
peaceably making their way to and from the
town centre, as if on a miniature version of the
famous Jesus Green in Cambridge, which lies
just twenty miles to the north.

At the far end of the town, overlooked by the
respectable Victorian villas at the privileged edge
of Saffron Walden's suburbs, is an unexpected
survival, thought to date back to Elizabethan
times – a turf maze. This consists of a narrow
path, now picked out in brick, in the form of
an intricate and pleasantly confusing doodle of
loops and concentric circles. If laid out straight,
it would stretch a mile, but here it is wound
tightly round itself into a circle of just one
hundred feet across: a small space, but easy
enough to get lost in.

*T*he town boasts hundreds of old houses, frequently
with jettied upper floors, like these examples along
Castle Street (right).

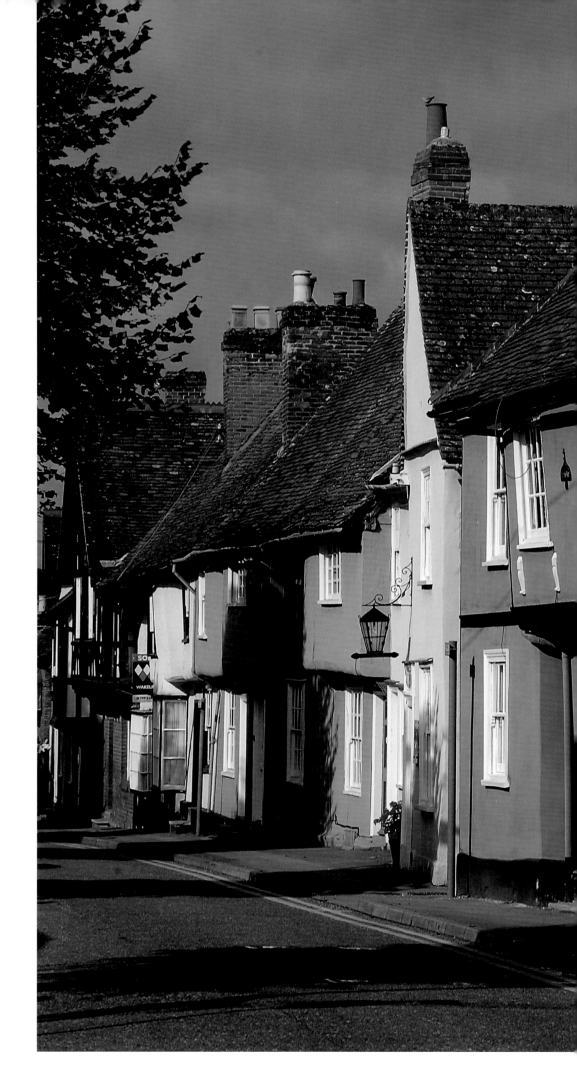

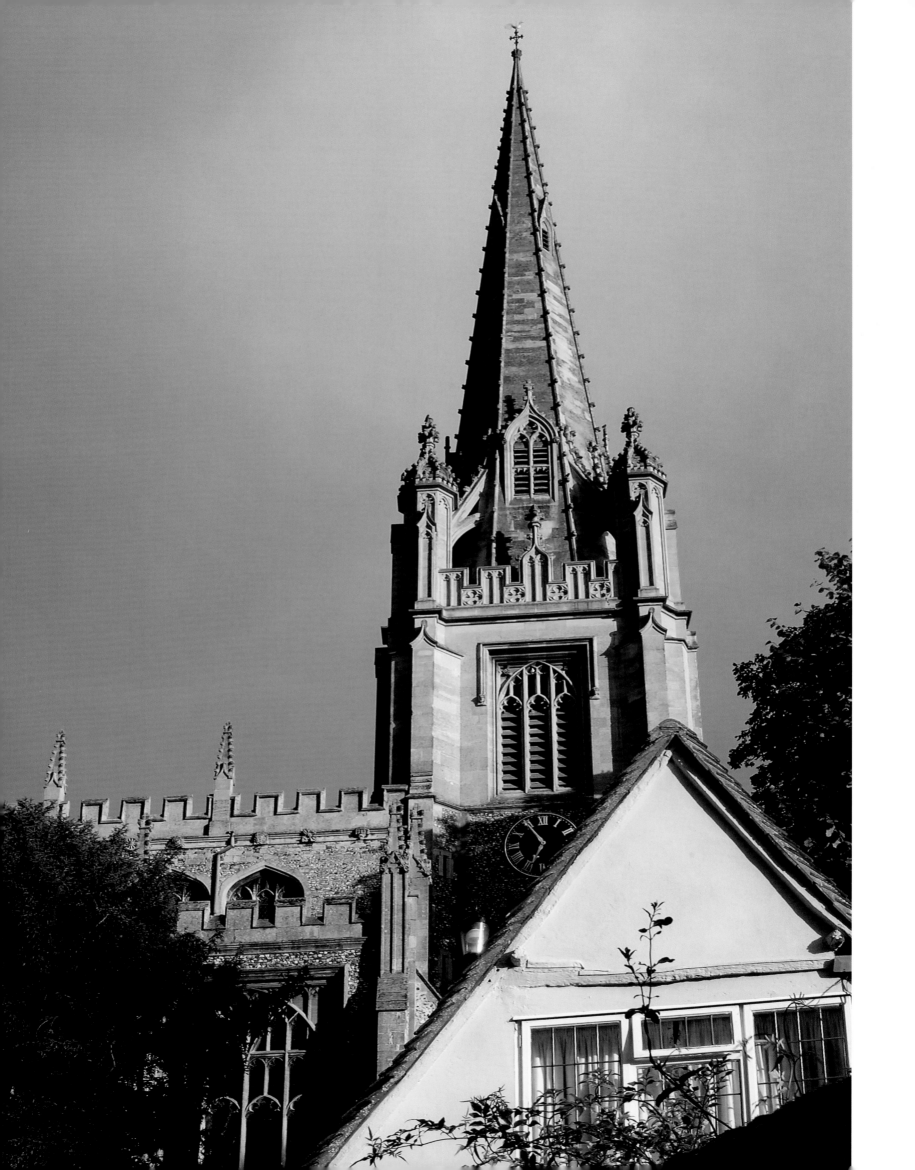

*I*n addition to its wealth of early
  domestic architecture, Saffron
Walden also has a number of more
elaborate structures, notably from
Victorian times (above *and* left).
A local speciality is the decorative
plasterwork known as pargeting (far
left). A mighty presence is the church
of St. Mary the Virgin (opposite),
the largest in the county, with a
mixture of Norman, Perpendicular
and Victorian elements.

*W*hatever the date or style, all the streets and buildings of Saffron Walden seem beautifully proportioned: Enson Close (above); the High Street (above right); by The Sun Inn of 1676 (right); the Italianate extravagance of the Corn Exchange (opposite).

A bench by the west porch of St. Mary the Virgin invites moments of contemplation and reflection (above).

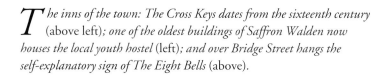

*T*he inns of the town: The Cross Keys dates from the sixteenth century
(above left); one of the oldest buildings of Saffron Walden now
houses the local youth hostel (left); and over Bridge Street hangs the
self-explanatory sign of The Eight Bells (above).

Stamford

LINCOLNSHIRE

THE ROMANS WERE the first road-builders to bypass Stamford. Their most vital north-south artery, connecting what was then Londinium with York, crossed the River Welland a few hundred yards west of the present Town Bridge. Of course, this was several hundred years before any settlement existed here, but Ermine Street was the forerunner of what later became known as the Great North Road. Stamford grew up at an important crossroads; the river itself was also a busy thoroughfare, connecting the East Midlands with the North Sea. By the thirteenth century Stamford had expanded to become one of the ten largest towns in England, complete with fourteen churches, a castle, two monasteries, four friaries, and even a short-lived university.

Happily, we can still enjoy the beauty of its architecture, harmoniously composed of the warm local limestone. Even as its mercantile importance dwindled, with the shift of the wool trade to the north, it became famous by association with a local man, William Cecil, who rose to be the first Queen Elizabeth's trusted chief minister. Cecil ended up an extremely wealthy man, and built his nobleman's palace, Burghley House, just outside the town. Many distinguished statesmen were to come from among his descendants, but his family was not greatly interested in Stamford's commercial independence, preferring to see it as an estate village on a grand scale. When the great era of coach travel came to an abrupt end, the town was left rather isolated, the more so when the Cecils succeeded in diverting the proposed Great Northern Railway to nearby Peterborough.

This, though, was all to Stamford's eventual gain, as will be appreciated by any traveller with the sense to turn off the thunderous A1, which now roars past the town (thankfully out of earshot). It is inspiring to look from St. Martin's church towards the river, imagining the horse-drawn coaches rattling down to The George Inn, against the pristine tableau of houses and churches rising up on the opposite bank.

*T*he view towards the steeple of the church of All Saints from the churchyard of St. Martin's (opposite) *may well have prompted Celia Fiennes in 1697 to this description of Stamford: 'as fine a built town all of stone as may be seen'. Later additions include a delicate chinoiserie porch on Barn Hill (above).*

*O*ld and not-so-old in Stamford: aged frontages in St. Paul's Street (opposite); the almshouses of Lord Burghley's Hospital (below), built on the site of the medieval Hospital of St. John; Rutland Terrace, speculative but attractive building of the 1820s (right).

The view from All Saints' churchyard (right) *in the centre of the town takes in the delightful domestic dwellings of All Saints' Street* (opposite).

*F*ull of picturesque details of all styles, Stamford never
fails to please: St. Peter's Hill (above); Rutland Terrace
(above right); and St. Paul's Street (right). Even the railway
station (opposite) has an otherworldly charm, perhaps a
reflection of the Cecil family succeeding in diverting the
Great Northern Railway to nearby Peterborough.

S tamford's great man: the memorial to William Cecil, first Lord Burghley, stands in St. Martin's church (above). But the most substantial memorial to the man who was Lord High Treasurer to Queen Elizabeth I is Burghley House (right), one of the great edifices of the Elizabethan era, set amid grounds landscaped in the late eighteenth century by 'Capability' Brown.

Almost concealed by trees, the church of St. Peter and St. Paul is just beyond the market-place (opposite). The domed Market Cross was donated by local townsfolk in 1783. An earlier benefactor, John Chapman, is commemorated in the wooden sign for the town (far right). Another reminder of the traditional prosperity of the town is this mid-Victorian decoration in brick on the Corn Exchange (right).

Swaffham
NORFOLK

AN EARLY AND fulsome enthusiast of Swaffham was William White, in whose 1844 Gazetteer its attractions are listed at length. He found it a 'handsome and thriving market-town', having 'a pleasant and highly salubrious situation on the crown of a lofty eminence', complete with 'gradually swelling acclivities'. Naturally, he records the appealing sobriquet that Swaffham had earned itself: 'the Montpelier of England'. Whether or not he was disingenuous in boosting the health benefits of spending time on an eminence that rises a modest fifty feet above the flat, fertile farmland of the Norfolk plain, he was certainly justified in pointing out the elegance of the place. By the time of his visit, Swaffham had become a smart social centre for the local gentry, who gathered to swap and generate gossip, and to marry off their daughters in a regular 'season', complete with a series of balls at the magnificent Assembly Rooms.

The Assembly Rooms still stand, while the immense scale of the broad square that they overlook does give a stately impression reminiscent of that of a classical French town. The size of the market-place has little to do with aesthetics, however. Swaffham became a very important commercial centre from the time King John granted the market its charter in 1216. Unlike some neighbouring towns such as Thetford, constrained by their closeness to a river, there was plenty of room for Swaffham to expand on its raised plateau, with ease of access to its market ensured by the broad streets that radiate from its centre. For centuries, it held the position of the premier cattle and corn market in the eastern counties. There used to be a thriving butter market there, too, under the shade of the domed lead roof of the fine Market Cross – appropriately topped with a figure of Ceres, goddess of plenty.

*J*ohn Chapman and his fellow merchants provided the means for building the town's magnificent Perpendicular church of St. Peter and St. Paul, complete with its hammer-beam ceiling (left *and* p.83). *The 'Gothick' lantern which crowns its tower (opposite) is a Georgian addition.*

A few miles to the north of Swaffham lies Castle Acre Priory (right), originally an offshoot of the great Benedictine abbey of Cluny in France and an important point on pilgrimage routes. The ruins include a fifteenth-century gatehouse, the prior's house, and the remains of a twelfth-century church.

Wisbech CAMBRIDGESHIRE

IF A NOTE of boastful defiance may be detected in Wisbech's self-conferred title, 'Capital of the Fens', a visit to this thinly populated stretch of north Cambridgeshire will make this understandable. Like Venice, which sits in similarly proud isolation on its inhospitable lagoon, the town can look back on a past of surprising mercantile power.

Its beginnings, however, were unpromising, situated as it was in an almost impenetrable fastness of misty salt marshland – the Fens. The great move to transform them into the orderly, productive landscape of today came in the seventeenth century, when engineers from the Netherlands brought their skills to the draining and dyke-building in the region. The vast resource of highly fertile land thus revealed had Wisbech as its natural centre. At the same time, the River Nene was diverted to its present, artificial course through the town. It established a link with The Wash to bring in shipping from abroad – in its heyday, the port was handling

70,000 tons of cargo each year. Celebrating the town's new mercantile wealth, two great rows of mansions were built facing each other across the Nene: North Brink and South Brink. Their elegance contrasts with the workmanlike appearance of the river itself; heavily tidal, its banks are deeply cut and often thickly coated with mud.

At the end of North Brink's graceful sweep sit the handsome Georgian premises of Elgood's Brewery, still very much in operation. Here are the original steaming copper vats, from which a large network of local pubs is supplied with beers tailored to meet the needs of the passing seasons. The inventive range includes Mad Dog, 'pale and fruity' to quench the thirst of the harvesters who still descend on Wisbech in midsummer, and the Wenceslas Winter Warmer, a 'rich red/brown distinctive warming brew' – ideal, no doubt, for fending off feelings of isolation during the long evenings of a chilly Fenland winter.

E vidence of the town's prosperity in Georgian times is everywhere present in Wisbech, like the houses of Union Place (opposite), built on the site of the town's former castle. More substantial houses line the North Brink and the South Brink along the banks of the River Nene (above).

*T*he North Brink's architectural treasures (above) *include the town hall* (to the right) *of 1801, part of which originally housed a poultry market and the local customs house. The town's main church* (above right *and* overleaf) *is notable for its double nave and detached tower with a peal of ten bells. Off the market-place elegant Georgian housing graces Chapel Road* (right), *while the pleasant period buildings of the grammar school, founded in 1549 by charter of Edward VI, lend distinction to the South Brink.*

*G*eorge Gilbert Scott designed this monument (right) on the Nene Quay in memory of Thomas Clarkson (1760–1846), a pioneer slave-trade abolitionist. Born in Wisbech, he was a pupil at the grammar school, where his father was headmaster.

The Southern Counties

*T*wo faces of Sussex: the traditional trappings of the English seaside holiday light up the East Parade in Hastings (above); Petworth (opposite) is one of the county's ancient market towns, mentioned in the Domesday Book.

IT IS DIFFICULT now to imagine what the southern counties looked like before the earliest humans arrived. Although the dry upland country was the first to be settled by Bronze Age tribes, and still holds many of the burial mounds that they left behind, there was never the wealth of natural resources to be found further north.

Surrey was once one of the least fortunate counties, with poor soil and a lack of building materials. Kent, Sussex and Hampshire had a better climate as well as access to the sea; the Romans were reputed to be the first to find that vines grew well there. Now, proximity to London has raised them all to become the richest part of the country – economically speaking, at least.

The idea that the southern counties have all disappeared under an ocean of tarmac is, happily, just a cartographic illusion and one easily disproved by the view from any aeroplane taking off from one of London's larger airports. The roads, a tangle of garish ribbons on a road map, quickly diminish in size, become as thin as threads, and then disappear – all that can be seen in almost any direction is a huge expanse of green fields and hedgerows. This vision is further sustained by expeditions on foot. The ancient ridgeways that run the length of the chalk Downs, for instance, are an excellent choice for walking: level, scenic and navigationally undemanding. At their eastern end they culminate, triumphantly, on that famous redoubt, the white cliffs of Dover.

Farnham SURREY

There is a neatness about the small-scale architecture of Farnham, typified by this seventeenth-century tile-hung example in Castle Street (above). A row of charming small cottages lines Church Lane on its way to St. Andrew's church (opposite).

IT WAS THE bishops of nearby Winchester who decided in the twelfth century that the small Saxon town of Farnham should be expanded. New land to the north of St. Andrew's church was laid out with spacious streets, and room for enough markets to satisfy the town's mercantile ambitions. The broad sweep of Castle Street, as it runs down to meet The Borough, Farnham's main street, is the most noble of the wide thoroughfares that typify many of England's market towns. The seventeenth-century author Daniel Defoe recounts meeting a local man who assured him that he had counted eleven hundred wagon-loads of grain coming to market there, in one day, although the resultant traffic jam must have been spectacular, even by Farnham standards.

Farnham is still a busy place. Despite the bypass to the south, which arrived after a very long and patient wait for the townspeople, there is plenty of through traffic coming from the north down Castle Hill and getting stuck in the one-way system. The pavements are busier still,

although there is space enough for shoppers to coexist fairly happily with the motorists.

Farnham owes its apparently charmed life to more than luck. One of the prosperous shopkeepers of late Victorian times and the early part of the twentieth century was a watchmaker and silversmith, Charles Borelli, who took a keen interest in the town's older buildings. He bought up a good deal of property in the town centre, and amused himself by remodelling it to his taste, aided by local architect Harold Falkner. Luckily his taste was sound, and he was an enthusiastic admirer of the Georgian style – fortunately, as Farnham's main streets are lined with the most wonderful collection of eighteenth-century houses.

Another inspiring incomer was the author and artist Sir John Verney, who came to live just outside Farnham after World War II. The disused Maltings down by the River Wey would have been flattened but for his vigorous campaign; they now house a thriving arts centre.

*T*he neo-Georgian colonnade of Farnham's town hall
looks out on to The Borough, the town's main street
(opposite). *Borelli's Yard (above) is one of the original
local coachyards, called after the Borelli family of
watchmakers, who did much to preserve the traditional
architecture of the town.*

*O*n top of Castle Hill stands
the gatehouse of what was
originally built as a palace for the
bishops of Winchester (opposite).
Another venerable brick edifice is
the row of Windsor Almhouses
(right), *built in 1619 for '8 poor,
honest, old and impotent persons'.*

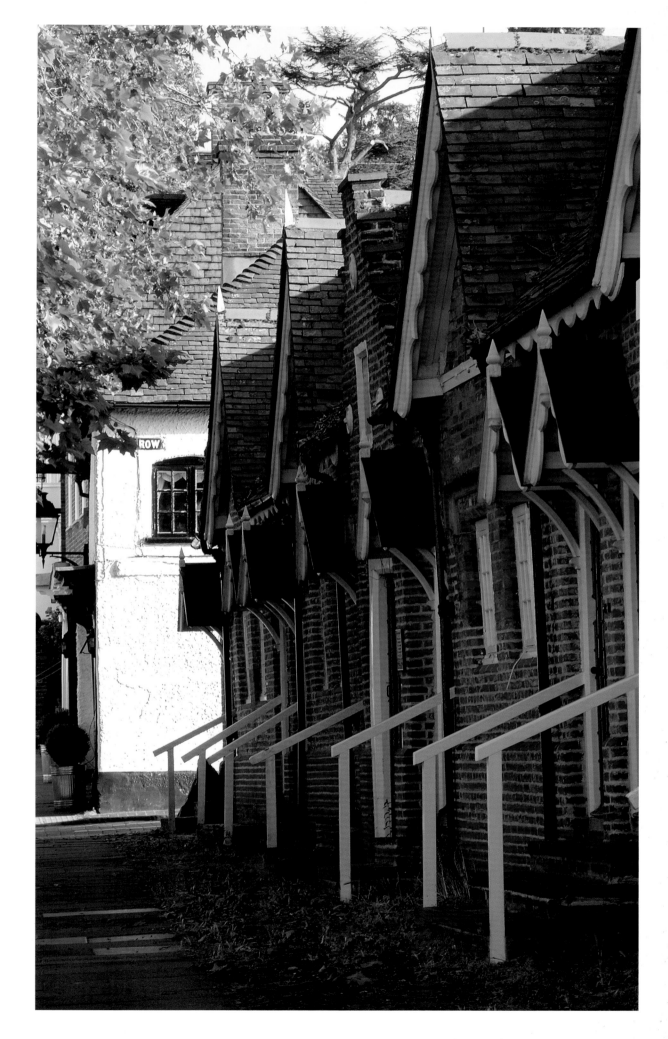

The houses along Castle Street (opposite and *this page) date from the mid-eighteenth century. One of them has become The Nelson Arms, indicated by a figure of the great naval hero.*

*T*he quality of life in the town
is expressed in fine detail: the
morning's milk delivery awaiting a
resident of Downing Street (far left);
a stylish entrance by the churchyard
(left); wall sculpture on the police
station (below); walking through
the Lion & Lamb Yard (opposite).

Faversham
KENT

AT FIRST SIGHT, Faversham hardly looks to be a port at all. Here are all the trappings of a successful market town, presided over by the fine Guildhall, still standing on its original sixteenth-century timber arcade. But just a short stroll away from here, Bridge Street slopes gently down from the market-place for only a hundred yards or so before it earns its name. The diminutive stream it crosses is none other than the famous Faversham Creek, which brought wealth to the town via its muddy meanderings towards the Swale estuary, and thereby to the great mouth of the Thames.

Amazingly, there was no other port that supplied seventeenth-century London with as much grain, and none other that exported more wool. Oysters and gunpowder also made their way from here, the latter manufactured locally in one of England's main ordnance mills. Inwards came pepper, tea, calico, tobacco. As an affiliate member of the Cinque Ports federation, Faversham enjoyed the privilege of running its own affairs in terms of taxes, tolls and even the administration of justice. Indeed, local enthusiasm for the town's freedoms seems to have exceeded respect for the law, as Daniel Defoe reported in his Tour of Great Britain in the 1720s: 'I know of nothing else the town is remarkable for, except the most notorious smuggling trade … in which they say the people hereabouts are arrived to such a proficiency, that they are grown monstrous rich…'. Nowadays the creek is all but silted up, and the last remaining boatyards look vulnerable to developers keen to create further 'desirable waterside properties', but the town's history has left behind it an unmistakable high-water mark of past affluence in its neat rows of Georgian houses, a picture of demure respectability.

*T*he Guildhall is still supported by the original octagonal columns that date from 1574 (opposite). Another important local landmark is the 1799 spire of the parish church of St. Mary of Charity (above).

*I*n keeping with the general architectural tone of the town
– exemplified in these restored houses (above *and* right)
on Abbey Street – is Faversham's 'Tudorbethan' cinema on
Middle Row (above right). The present Ship Hotel (opposite)
has a fine eighteenth-century frontage.

Since the 16th Century when Henry VIIIs fleet lay at anchor in Faversham Creek, an Inn has stood on this site. Originally a simple wine tavern called "The Shippe", over the centuries the enlarged "Ship Inn" became an important stagecoach stop between London and Dover. All kinds of coaches and carriages, bringing travellers, revenue and excise men, military officers, couriers, merchants and humble journeymen passed beneath this archway.

THE SHIP

SHIP

CLOSED

*T*raditional weatherboarding (opposite) *adds a distinctive note to a number of the older houses of the town, including those in* Partridge Lane (above). Abbey Street (right) *has more of Faversham's charming domestic architecture.*

*F*aversham's Guildhall (right) had to be rebuilt after a disastrous fire in 1814, caused by locals celebrating one of Wellington's victories. But present-day Court Street (below) looks peaceful enough. The Faversham Creek (opposite) recalls the town's previous importance as a port; it is still deep enough to accommodate traditional sailing barges.

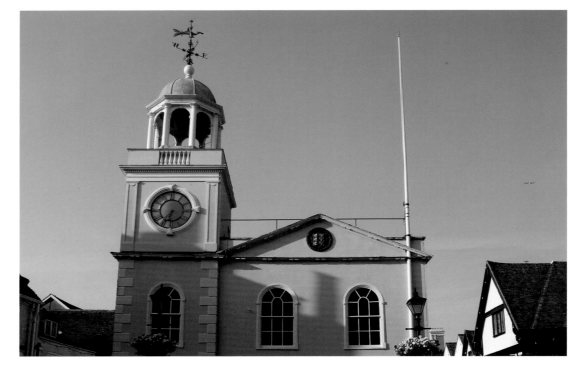

Hastings EAST SUSSEX

*T*he elongated forms of the net-
drying huts (above) *give a
distinctive look to The Stade, the
shingle beach of the town. Now an
arts centre, the church of St. Mary-
in-the-Castle is a neoclassical high
note at the centre of Pelham
Crescent* (opposite).

LIKE ITS NEIGHBOURS along the coast, Hastings
has its share of fancy sea-front terraces, built by
speculators keen to cash in on the Regency vogue
for sea-bathing. But unlike Brighton, whose
fashionable splendour belied its humble origins
as the fishing village of Brighthelmston, Hastings
was already a town of substance. For some time
it was the most important of the Cinque Ports,
especially after the other founder members were
left high and dry by the movement outwards
of the coast. This has never been Hastings'
problem – indeed its troubled relationship with
the sea, its devastating storms and ever-shifting
shingle, put paid to many attempts to build a
harbour there.

The seaside amenities were built to last,
however; there is certainly nothing insubstantial
about the spacious promenade that leads
eastwards from the pier, towards the Old Town.
Here the view seawards is blocked by an
amusement park, but anyone who finds the

polychromatic charms of Playland too much
may discover relief in the weather-boarded,
tar-daubed buildings which seem to owe their
elongated, tottering shapes to the fairground
mirrors on the nearby pier. This is The Stade,
the old fishing quarter, and these are the net
stores, and almost more extraordinary, here are
the fishing-boats themselves, pulled up on the
shingle. These stubby, clinker-built 'luggers' are
part of the fishing fleet that has been launched
from this beach for the past thousand years.
There is a ready market for the day's catch,
particularly among the day-trippers who still
come down from London by the coachload.

The traditional English holiday-maker is a
dwindling resource, however. But happily, the
tidal flow of fashion is coming to Hastings'
rescue once more. The smart money is pouring
in, as a new generation of young professionals
falls for the raffish charm of the town, preferring
it to the expensive gentility of Brighton.

*A*ll Saints' Street (above), *the main thoroughfare of the Old Town, is notable for its exceptionally well-preserved old houses.*

*T*he town has a slightly worn, raffish charm about it
(above left *and* left). *And if the foot-weary visitor
still wishes to enjoy the view from the upper reaches, then
there is always the East Hill Lift (above) to hand – one
of two cliff railways.*

*T*he Stade (above) *and the* Old Town (above
right *and* right) *offer pleasures both culinary and
architectural to the many day-trippers who still visit
Hastings. One of the delights in store is to sample the
catch from the beach fishing-boats which are still
launched from the shingle of* The Stade (opposite).

*Pages 148–49 A spacious and substantial promenade
leads from the pier, first opened in 1872 and modelled
on the West Pier at Brighton.*

Lymington
HAMPSHIRE

By DETACHING ITSELF from the English mainland at the end of the last Ice Age, the Isle of Wight created an ideal base for the country's shipping activities. The River Solent, protected from adverse weather as well as unexpected attack, became the chief thoroughfare of a world-dominating navy. But it was not always the massive harbours of Portsmouth and Southampton from which it set forth. These only developed after ships became too large to use the little estuaries where the earliest ports grew up. Lymington was one of them, trading in locally produced salt and building its own wooden boats in a distinctive style. The neighbouring estuary to the east, that of the even tinier River Beaulieu, was where much of Nelson's navy was constructed.

Lymington is still a busy port, its small scale ideal for the comings and goings of yachtsmen. They can berth at the town's historic dock, then make their way up Quay Hill, cobbled and lined with bow-windowed shops, to the start of the High Street. Wide and stately, this leads between rows of distinctive shops and houses towards the proud, cupola-topped tower of St. Thomas the Apostle.

Lymington's continuing charm owes much to the surrounding New Forest, a protective cushion of ancient heath and woodland that insulates it from the less agreeable qualities of the overcrowded south. The motorway that thunders past Ringwood can encroach no closer; access is only by tranquil, leafy (and, in summer, very slow-moving) lanes. So, the second most pleasant way to arrive in the town is by train. An obliging branch line chugs steadily through the tranquillity of the Forest before terminating at Lymington's two miniscule stations: Lymington Town and, a hundred or so yards further on, Lymington Pier. From here, a regular ferry service is available to whisk the yachtless across the Solent to the Isle of Wight's oldest harbour – Yarmouth.

The estuary of the River Lymington is home to a number of ocean-going pleasure craft (right).

The cobblestones of Quay Hill (above) lead up from Lymington's quayside to the town's High Street. Lined with elegant, bow-fronted shops and restaurants, this is, enjoyably, an entirely pedestrianized thoroughfare.

This handsome house in the town's High Street (left) has been embellished with an especially fine balcony rail. More modest dwellings line the distinctly maritime Captain's Row (below) in the quayside area. The name underlines the town's close connections with the sea; and Lymington still remains an important base for yachts and yacht-building.

*I*t is hard to avoid encountering at any time some utterly charming corner or feature in Lymington, many of them, though not all, connected directly with the maritime life: one of the two sailing clubs of the town (above); a waterside pub on The Quay (opposite above left); the church of St. Thomas, a focal point for the High Street (opposite above right); the crinkle-crankle wall of Grove Place, on Church Lane (opposite below).

Petworth WEST SUSSEX

*T*he stone and brick tower of St. Mary's church (opposite) entices the visitor up the gentle slope of Lombard Street, generally agreed to be the town's prettiest, although Grove Street (above) also has its obvious charms.

IN FRANCE IT is not at all unusual to see a château and its dependent houses co-existing cheek by jowl in the centre of a country town. Frequently, the local population relied on the stronghold for protection, and could retire behind its walls in times of danger. In contrast to such arrangements, Petworth's setting, on a gentle ridge a few miles north of the chalk Downs, looks far too peaceful to suggest any danger of war or siege, its layout being more a matter of domestic convenience for the noble inhabitants of Petworth House. Indeed, much of the town was in its ownership as a convenient dormitory for the armies of retainers. The House itself presents its reverse to the town; its true magnificence is oriented in the opposite direction, where the West Front, whose grandeur would have impressed even a French king, looks over a matchless landscaped setting, the creation of Lancelot 'Capability' Brown.

The town itself does not suffer overmuch from its intimacy with the House. Admittedly, it presents itself unsatisfactorily to the motorist, who must drive through Petworth, squeezing along the edge of the House, navigating a series of sharp corners round the high walls and unprepossessing outbuildings. But to the visitor on foot, it reveals itself as a jewel-box of delights, the more beguiling for its modest scale.

Despite its grand title, the High Street consists of a charming collection of domestic cottages. There are a few large buildings, such as the grandiose Town Hall, donated by the third Earl of Egremont in 1793. Every 20 November, it looks disdainfully over a scene of dodgem cars and merry-go-rounds, as the street fair, an annual tradition since 1189, manages to squeeze its attractions into the miniature Market Square.

*P*etworth is a town arranged around a great house that turns its back to the surrounding habitations (above), *seen here from the churchyard of St. Mary's. But there are plenty of more modest details for the visitor to enjoy: at the back of Pound Street* (opposite above left); *off Lombard Street* (opposite left).

*N*ot everything in the town is dependent on Petworth House; many of the streets boast interesting buildings in a variety of architectural styles and materials (these pages).

The Western Counties

The counties of the west of England have traditional associations with myth, legend and alternative culture: a shop (above) selling mystical artifacts in Totnes, Devonshire. They are also famous for their landscapes: the view from Park Walk (opposite) in Shaftesbury, Dorset.

ENGLAND'S WEST COUNTRY is, at least in popular imagination, the country's wellspring and repository of its most enduring myths and legends. Perhaps this is because of its strong association with the Celtic tribes, for whom poetry and magic were at the heart of their culture. They once ruled most of England, but were forced back by the Roman legions to form their last strongholds in the West. Pragmatically, the invaders did not choose to pursue them into the wilder reaches of the Cornish peninsula, satisfied as they were by the riches they discovered in Dorset and Somerset. This productive arable land was to provide much of the huge wealth accumulated by the great abbeys, such as those of Glastonbury and Shaftesbury, and by the towns that they supported. Later, but before the power of the monks had been swept away, it was the turn of the less productive downland of Wiltshire; the sheep that grazed there enabled towns such as Bradford-on-Avon to become prosperous centres of wool trading and weaving. A plentiful supply of local limestone enabled merchants and artisans to create the harmonious townscape that rises up the steep banks of the river.

What Devonshire and Cornwall lack in arable wealth, they make up for in building resources. Fine stone abounds, especially deep into Cornwall, where granite church towers rise between the steep curves of the hillsides. The countryside of Devonshire is cosier, more genteel, although the huge desolate massif of Dartmoor, which rises to as great a height as the Peak District of Derbyshire, lies within its borders. Certainly there is gentility to be found on Devonshire's south coast, where the benign effect of the Gulf Stream has created a string of seaside resorts, complete with palm trees – the 'English Riviera'.

The Cornish coast is wilder, facing off the increasing might of the Atlantic Ocean as it tapers to a dramatic finale at Lizard Point and Land's End. On the north coast, St. Ives has for many centuries sheltered fishing fleets behind the crook of its foreland. From there, rocky coves alternate with sandy beaches all the way to Tintagel and its fairy-tale castle. The legend of King Arthur seems naturally at home in the West Country; Tintagel is claimed to be his birthplace, while his remains are said to lie in the abbey grounds at Glastonbury.

Bradford-on-Avon
WILTSHIRE

'A STRONG AND HANDSOME bridge, in the middest of which is a little chapell for masse as at Bathe…'. It is no surprise that Bradford-on-Avon reminded John Aubrey of the great city that lies just over the border in Somerset, only eight miles distant. Bradford shares the same beautiful, warm limestone, and even by 1660, when the Wiltshire antiquary was writing, the stately ranks of houses would already have been rising up the steep wooded banks of the River Avon.

This was a crossing-place from the earliest times; the town's name comes from the 'Broad Ford' that was used before the first bridge was built. It was not only the ready supply of Bath stone that caused the houses to be so fine, and the bridge so grand; Bradford was also a major centre of cloth manufacture, using the wool from the Wiltshire downs and even attracting craftsmen from the Low Countries, brought over to introduce improved techniques of weaving and spinning. The artisans would have lived and worked in the terraces of the smaller houses that balance, apparently on top of one another, on the steeper slopes. These were generally built from rubble - the loose, irregular stone from the quarries. The carefully cut blocks of stone were reserved for their employers, the wealthy clothiers, whose mansions were built to rival the grandeur of Bath. The river played an active part in the development of the town; by the early nineteenth century, there were no fewer than thirty-two mills along its banks. Shortly afterwards, though, the wool industry moved abruptly to the mills of the north, bringing huge wealth to Bradford's Yorkshire namesake.

Today, the town looks to be thriving, even without having to produce anything; the remaining mills have been snapped up by apartment-dwellers, who can now own a desirable outlook over the Town Bridge, still strong and handsome, but with its chapel converted in the seventeenth century into the town's 'Blind House' – its picturesque lock-up.

The tiny chapel on the Town Bridge (left) was rebuilt in the seventeenth century as the 'Blind House', a lock-up for unruly townsfolk.

As a crossing-place over the Avon, the town enjoyed some importance from earliest times, testimony to which is this nave of the Anglo-Saxon church of St. Lawrence's (left). Evidence of later prosperity, derived from the wool industry, lies in the terraces which rise up the steep slopes of the river valley (opposite); this one, known as 'Tory', adjoins the tiny church of St. Mary Tory.

A sense of the past is promptly evoked by the town's street names – Market Street and The Shambles (these pages).

Well-used premises on Silver Street (opposite) offer the time-honoured services of shoe-mending and key-cutting. Two steep parallel streets, Coppice Hill and Whitehead's Lane (above and left), climb up from Silver Street, once named Market Place and the site of a former town hall.

Mellow Bath stone lends its warmth to the buildings along the Avon (above) and to the fine houses of Tory (left). The Abbey Mill (opposite), the last of Bradford's working mills to close, has now been converted into apartments.

Glastonbury SOMERSET

A discreet gate opens from the Abbey precincts to Silver Street behind; close by rises the Perpendicular tower of St. John's on the High Street (above). The Abbey barn (opposite) is a marvellous example of fourteenth-century craftsmanship in its 'cruck' construction.

THE ABBEY AT Glastonbury, around whose remains the town still clusters, was one of the greatest and earliest of English monastic sites. Myths abound concerning its origins. According to legend, it was Joseph of Arimathaea who first founded a church there, accompanied, according to some variants, by his nephew Jesus Christ, making an undocumented excursion to England. Joseph's association with the Holy Grail certainly did no harm to Glastonbury's reputation as a centre for pilgrimage, which was further boosted by the discovery, in 1191, of two bodies said to be those of King Arthur and his Queen Guinevere.

The rich agricultural lands that the monks developed so successfully (theirs was the first organized attempt to drain the substantial area of wetland between the Quantocks and the Mendips known as the Somerset Levels) stood the town in good stead after King Henry VIII brought the influence of the monasteries to an end. Appropriately, the ancient business of welcoming

pilgrims has undergone a recent revival; each year the Glastonbury Festival draws in devotees of a New Age by the thousand. Many of them are so deeply attracted to the place that they stay year-round, as is apparent from the succession of wholefood cafes and tantric emporia which have sprung up along the High Street, to the bemusement of the older townsfolk.

One feature towers above the swirling mists of Glastonbury folklore. The conical hill, or 'Tor', that rises abruptly just to the east of the town, is a true natural curiosity. It looks so like a burial mound, despite its improbable scale, that the very notion that it was put there by nature can set the most down-to-earth visitor off on a magical train of thought. Or, gazing across the flat, once inundated countryside below, one might muse on the practical attraction it once held for the first human inhabitants, impelled by that most universal longing – keeping dry.

*R*eligious and architectural tradition
mingle with New Age interests on the
High Street (above *and* above right). *A more
conventional spirituality is represented by the
thirteenth-century chapel of St. Mary's
Almshouses, off Magdalene Street (right).*

*T*he fifteenth-century Tribunal (above), *a Gothic stone house originally built for use by the Abbey, is now home to the Tourist Information Office.*

T his view of the Abbey remains (right) shows the Lady Chapel, as we look through the nave towards the high altar.

Shaftesbury
DORSET

'VAGUE IMAGININGS OF its castle, its three mints, its magnificent Abbey…its twelve churches, its shrines, chantries, hospitals…all now ruthlessly swept away, throw the visitor into a pensive melancholy.' Thus wrote Thomas Hardy, the celebrated author of Dorset, on the despoiling of Shaftesbury. He was well known as an unsparing critic of his own, industrial age, but here, surprisingly, it was the Georgians who were the culprits. Only the barest fragments survive of what was once the most powerful Benedictine nunnery in the country, and one of great antiquity, having first been founded by King Alfred for his daughter. Of the castle, at the west end of the spur on which the town stands, nothing remains at all.

The majority of visitors, who may not have read their Hardy, will find the absence of Shaftesbury's ancient treasures so complete that they will be able to enjoy it for what it is now: an unassuming market town, blessed with something that time can never take away – a glorious position. From its commanding spur, some seven hundred feet in height, two fine promenades give wonderful views over green expanses of countryside. From Park Walk, which backs on to the Abbey ruins, one looks south over Dorset; from Castle Hill at the other end of town, the view is towards neighbouring Wiltshire.

As a finale, a pilgrimage can be made to an important monument to contemporary culture. From St. Peter's in the High Street, the one remaining medieval church of the original twelve, a narrow passage leads to the top of Gold Hill, where a row of perfect, modest cottages, stepping down the steep, cobbled slope, face the old buttressed walls of the Abbey grounds. Confronted with this quintessentially English scene, an emotion of half-forgotten familiarity may be evoked and possibly lead on to a pensive melancholy of a modern kind; this was, after all, the location for the long-running, hugely successful and very sentimental television commercial for Hovis, a factory-made bread.

A row of stone cottages (right) *tumbles down Shaftesbury's famous Gold Hill beneath the buttressed retaining wall of the Abbey precinct.*

A *quiet, unassuming market town: these scenes (above and* right) *of Shaftesbury's High Street capture the essence of the place.*

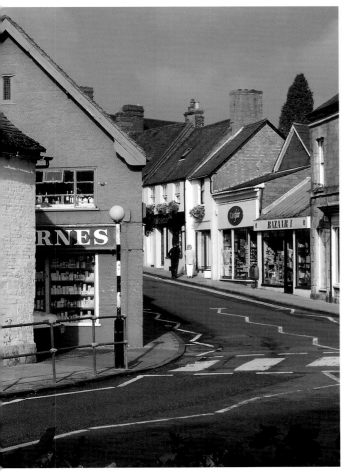

*A*s well as having generally agreeable streets (above left *and* left), *Shaftesbury has a number of notable buildings. These include an early George Gilbert Scott design* (opposite left) *and the intriguing town hall* (above) *at the top of the High Street, built in the Tudor style but dating in fact from the 1820s.*

Overleaf *Park Walk offers this fine view over the Dorset countryside.*

St. Ives
CORNWALL

ESPECIALLY ON A fine sunny day in summer, St. Ives looks cheerful and relaxed in its present role as holiday resort and long-suffering artists' model. The town's characterful appearance reflects the mixture of traditional skills – fishing, mining and farming (not to speak of smuggling) – that kept it flourishing in the past. It perches on the rocky headland that shelters its harbour, a safe haven on the rugged and often weather-beaten north coast of Cornwall. It can easily accommodate the few remaining fishing-boats which now share it with pleasure and tour craft. At the landward end of Smeaton's Pier the diminutive St. Leonard's Chapel still stands. Here the fishermen used to seek God's blessing before setting out. On their safe return, the Almighty's representative on earth would receive his slice of the action, paid in fish. In the happy era of abundant pilchard, the fishermen used to lie in wait for passing shoals, which were scooped up in a giant seine a quarter of a mile long, to be brought ashore, barrelled in salt and shipped out again. Some of the packing sheds where this doubtless malodorous operation used to take place still exist, on the seaward side of the intricate warren of passageways and cottages that rises up from the main harbour. This fishermen's quarter, known as 'Downalong', was where the artists who came to frequent St. Ives used to have their studios. Present-day artists, who still come in great numbers, can enjoy the wonderful prevailing light, with nothing more to distract them than the healthy tang of sea air. The best of their work can be enjoyed in the delightful new seaside annexe to the Tate Gallery, which sits right on the beach-front, its minimalist spaces radiant with the light peculiar to north coasts.

Tate Gallery St. Ives (above) opened in 1993, a testament to the town's importance as a centre for contemporary painting and sculpture. The harbour (opposite) is now home to relatively few fishing-boats, but in the past it had to be enlarged to accommodate the massive pilchard fleet.

*T*he beach along The Wharf (opposite), *exposed at low tide, is shared between boats and sunbathers. Behind The Wharf is the warren of lanes, lined with fishermen's cottages* (this page), *which proved such an attraction for the first arrivals of what was to become a flourishing artists' colony.*

*I*n the past, all the wheeled traffic to the harbour had to pass through the
narrow streets of the town's old centre (above left *and* right). *A passing
surfer reminds us that art is not the only concern of the town. Nevertheless,
it is perhaps its major concern and nowhere more so than at the Barbara
Hepworth Museum (opposite), consisting of the sculptor's studio and
garden. It has been maintained by the Tate Gallery sine 1980.*

*T*he oldest part of St. Ives rises up beyond the harbour, now more a centre for holiday-makers rather than a working fishing port (right). Further away is the rocky headland known as The Island, a favourite spot for birdwatchers and yielding spectacular views.

Totnes
DEVONSHIRE

MYTHS ABOUND IN the West Country. Perhaps it is part of the fanciful legacy left behind by the Celtic tribes – this was their last stronghold before the more prosaic Anglo-Saxons drove them out in the sixth century. Totnes, however, can boast a mythical provenance that goes back further still. The fortunate town, and with it the whole of Britain, was allegedly founded by a wandering prince named Brutus, said to have arrived in the town after the destruction of his native Troy.

The visitor who stands on the east bank of the River Dart and looks across at Totnes will feel no need for so fanciful an explanation of the town's beginnings. This is a perfect crossing-point over the river, and an ideal terminus for the river traffic that still makes its way through the tortuous estuary of the Dart. Pleasure yachts berth here now, but these quays were formerly the scene of constant activity, as ships were loaded with cloth and tin from Dartmoor, returning from France with canvas and wine.

A steep walk from the river takes the visitor under the restored arch-house of the East Gate into the oldest part of the town. As the view-point changes, the Norman castle at the top of the hill disappears among the closely set old houses, as does the red-stone tower of the parish church, that sails so prominently above the town when viewed from the opposite side of the river. Now St. Mary's reappears in its own little close, set back from the street, in the shelter of the castle itself. On the way up, there is a pleasing assortment of old houses, some hung with tiles, some timbered. Set into the pavement outside 51 Fore Street is a reminder of that happy day in 1170 B.C.: the very lump of granite on to which the Trojan made his historic landfall.

*I*n the upper part of the town the High Street presents an interesting mixture of building styles and materials (right) *against the castellated backdrop of the town's ancient castle.*

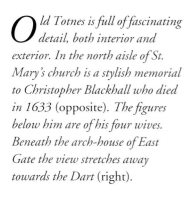

*O*ld Totnes is full of fascinating detail, both interior and exterior. In the north aisle of St. Mary's church is a stylish memorial to Christopher Blackhall who died in 1633 (opposite). *The figures below him are of his four wives. Beneath the arch-house of East Gate the view stretches away towards the Dart* (right).

*G*limpses of old Totnes (this page) *include*
interestingly converted former fishing stores. And
along the river there are more conversions of former
warehouses (opposite).

*T*he countryside south-west of Totnes (overleaf) *is*
a mixture of downland and wooded valleys – here,
that of the River Erme.

SCOTLAND

North Sea

□ BERWICK-UPON-TWEED

● *Alnwick*

□ NEWCASTLE-UPON-TYNE

Barnard Castle ●
□ DARLINGTON

Ambleside ●

□ KENDAL

The Northern Counties

Irish Sea

Lancaster ●

● *Beverley*

BLACKBURN □

□ HALIFAX

MANCHESTER □

□ SHEFFIELD

Buxton ●

The Midland Counties

□ NEWARK
NOTTINGHAM □

The Eastern Counties

Swaffham ●

Stamford ●   *Wisbech* ●

□ NORWICH

Bridgnorth ●   BIRMINGHAM □

W A L E S

Ludlow ●

NORTHAMPTON □

CAMBRIDGE □   *Bury St. Edmunds* ●

Stratford-upon-Avon ●

Chipping Campden ●

LUTON ●   *Saffron Walden* ●

COLCHESTER □

HEREFORD □

GLOUCESTER □

□ OXFORD

READING □

LONDON ●

The Southern Counties

Faversham ●

BATH ●   *Bradford-on-Avon* ●

Glastonbury ●

GUILDFORD □

FOLKESTONE □

BARNSTAPLE □

Farnham ●

□ TAUNTON

Shaftesbury ●   *Petworth* ●   *Hastings* ●

The Western Counties

DORCHESTER □   *Lymington* ●

Totnes ●   □ TORQUAY

□ TRURO

St. Ives ●

English Channel

A Travellers' Guide

While every effort has been made to ensure that the information given in the following entries is correct, the author and the publisher cannot be held responsible for any inadvertent inaccuracies.

The Northern Counties

Alnwick, Northumberland

Tourist Information Centre, 2 The Shambles, NE66 1TN, 01665 510665

WHERE TO STAY
White Swan Hotel, 16 Bondgate Within, NE66 1TD, 01665 602109
Bondgate House, 20 Bondgate Without, NE66 1PN, 01665 602025
Roseworth, Alnmouth Road, NE66 2PR, 01665 603911
Tower Restaurant & Accommodation, 10 Bondgate Within, NE66 1TD, 01665 603888

WHERE TO EAT
Tower Restaurant & Accommodation, 10 Bondgate Within, NE66 1TD, 01665 603888
Queen's Head Hotel, 25 Market Street, NE66 1SS, 01665 604691

Ambleside, Cumbria

Tourist Information Centre, Central Buildings, Market Cross, LA22 9BS, 015394 32582

WHERE TO STAY
Grey Friar Lodge Country House Hotel, Clappersgate, LA22 9NE, 015394 33158
Brathay Lodge, Rothay Road, LA22 0EE, 015394 32000
Chapel House Bed & Breakfast, Kirkstone Road, LA22 9DZ, 015394 33143
Compston House American Style Bed & Breakfast, Compston Road, LA22 9DJ, 015394 32305
Ambleside Backpackers, Old Lake Road, LA22 0DJ 015394 32340

WHERE TO EAT
Zeffirelli's Pizzeria, Millans Park, LA22 9AD, 015394 33845
Glass House Restaurant, Rydal Road, LA22 9AN, 015394 32137

Barnard Castle, Co. Durham

Tourist Information Centre, Woodleigh, Flatts Road, DL12 8AA, 01833 690909

WHERE TO STAY
Montalbo Hotel, 84 Montalbo Road, DL12 8BP, 01833 637342
The Old Well Inn, 21 The Bank, DL12 8PH, 01833 690 130
Number 34, 34 The Bank, DL12 8PN, 01833 631304

WHERE TO EAT
Blagraves House Restaurant, 30–32 The Bank, DL12 8PN, 01833 637668
The Market Place Teashop, 29 Market Place, DL12 8NE, 01833 690110

Beverley, East Riding of Yorkshire

Tourist Information Centre, 34 Butcher Row, HU17 0AB, 01482 867430

WHERE TO STAY
Beverley Arms Hotel, North Bar Within, HU17 8DD, 01482 869241
Eastgate Guesthouse, 7 Eastgate, HU17 0DR, 01482 868464
North Bar Lodge, 28 North Bar Without, HU17 7AB, 01482 881375

WHERE TO EAT
Cerutti 2, Station Square, HU17 0AS, 01482 866700
Gingers, 1 Swabys Yard, Walkergate, HU17 9BZ, 01482 882919

Lancaster, Lancashire

Tourist Information Centre, 29 Castle Hill, LA1 1YN, 01524 32878

WHERE TO STAY
Edenbreck House, Sunnyside Lane, LA1 5AD, 01524 32464
Royal Kings Arms Hotel, Market Street, LA1 1JG, 01773 829133
Old Station House, 25 Meeting House Lane, LA1 1TX, 01524 381060
Wagon & Horses, 27 St. George's Quay, LA1 1RD, 01524 846094
WHERE TO EAT
Simply French, 27a St. George's Quay, LA1 1RD, 01524 843199
Sun Café, Sun Street Studios, 25 Sun Street, LA1 1EW, 01524 845599

The Midland Counties

Bridgnorth, Shropshire

Tourist Information Centre, Listley Street, WV16 4AW, 01746 763257

WHERE TO STAY
The Croft Hotel, St. Mary's Street, WV16 4DW, 01746 762416
The Golden Lion, 83 High Street, WV16 4DS, 01746 762016
Severn Arms Hotel, Underhill Street, WV16 4BB, 01746 764616
Parlors Hall Hotel, Mill St, WV15 5AL, 01746 761931
WHERE TO EAT
The Habit Restaurant & Bar, 30–32 East Castle Street, WV16 4AN, 01746 767902
Bassa Villa Bar & Grill, 48 Cartway, WV16 4BG, 01746 763977

Buxton, Derbyshire

Tourist Information Centre, The Crescent, SK17 6BQ, 01298 25106

WHERE TO STAY
Old Hall Hotel & Restaurant, The Square, SK17 6AL, 01298 22841
Palace Hotel, Palace Road, SK17 6AG, 01298 22001
Buxton's Victorian Guest House, 3a Broad Walk, SK17 6JE, 01298 78759
Grendon Guest House, Bishops Lane, SK17 6UN, 01298 78831
Netherdale Guest House, 16 Green Lane, SK17 9DP, 01298 23896
Stoneridge Guest House, 9 Park Road, SK17 6SG, 01298 26120
WHERE TO EAT
Columbine Restaurant, 7 Hall Bank, SK17 6EW, 01298 78752
The Hydro Tea Rooms, 75 Spring Gardens, SK17 6BP, 01298 79065

Chipping Campden, Gloucestershire

Tourist Information Centre, The Old Police Station, High Street, GL55 6HB, 01386 841206

WHERE TO STAY
Noel Arms Hotel, High Street, GL55 6AT, 01386 840317
Cotswold House, The Square, GL55 6AN, 01386 840330
Kings Arms, The Square, GL55 6AW, 01386 840256
Badgers Hall, High Street, GL55 6HB, 01386 840839
Weston Park Farm, Dovers Hill, GL55 6UW, 01386 840835
WHERE TO EAT
Juliana's Restaurant, Cotswold House, The Square, GL55 6AN, 01386 840330
The Eight Bells Inn, Church Street, GL55 6JG, 01386 840371

Ludlow, Shropshire

Tourist Information Centre, Castle Street, SY8 1AS, 01584 875053

WHERE TO STAY
The Feathers Hotel, Bull Ring, SY8 1AA, 01584 875261
Church Inn, Buttercross, SY8 1AW, 01584 872174
The Wheatsheaf Inn, Lower Broad Street, SY8 1PQ, 01584 872980
Number 28, 28 Lower Broad Street, SY8 1PQ, 01584 876996
Bromley Court, 73/74 Lower Broad Street, SY8 1PH, 01584 876996
WHERE TO EAT
Merchant House, 62 Lower Corve Street, SY8 1DU, 01584 875438
Hibiscus Restaurant, 17 Corve Street, SY8 1DA, 01584 872325
Koo Japanese Restaurant, 127 Old Street, SY8 1NU, 01584 878462

Stratford-upon-Avon, Warwickshire

Tourist Information Centre, Bridgefoot, CV37 6GW, 01789 293127

WHERE TO STAY
The Shakespeare Hotel, Chapel Street, CV37 6ER, 01789 294771
The Payton, 6 John Street, CV37 6UB, 01789 266442
Woodstock Guest House, 30 Grove Road, CV37 6PB, 01789 299881
Parkfield, 3 Broad Walk, CV37 6HS, 01789 293313
Arden Park 'Non-Smoking' Hotel, 6 Arden St, CV37 6PA, 01789 296072
WHERE TO EAT
Lambs of Sheep Street, 12 Sheep Street, CV37 6EF, 01789 292554
Russons Restaurant, 8 Church Street, CV37 6HB, 01789 268822
Margaux, 6 Union Street, CV37 6QT, 01789 269106

The Eastern Counties

Bury St. Edmunds, Suffolk

Tourist Information Centre, 6 Angel Hill, IP33 1UZ, 764667

WHERE TO STAY
The Angel, 3 Angel Hill, IP33 1LT, 01284 714000
Ounce House, 13–14 Northgate Street, IP33 1HP, 01284 761779
South Hill House, 43 Southgate Street, IP33 2AZ, 01284 755650
Northgate House, 8 Northgate Street, IP33 1HQ, 01284 760469
WHERE TO EAT
Maison Bleue, 30-31 Churchgate Street, IP33 1RG, 01284 760623

Saffron Walden, Essex

Tourist Information Centre, 1 Market Place, CB10 1HR, 01799 510444

WHERE TO STAY
The Saffron Hotel, 10–12 High Street, CB10 1AZ, 01799 522676
Cross Keys Hotel, 32 High Street, CB10 1AX, 01799 522207
Cromwell Lodge, 10 Common Hill, CB10 1JG, 01799 527 640
Oak House, 40 Audley Road, CB11 3HD, 01799 523 290
WHERE TO EAT
Eight Bells, 18 Bridge Street, CB10 1BU, 01799 522790
Dish Restaurant and Bars, 13A King Street, CB10 1HE, 01799 513300
Maze Coffee Shop, 9 Market Place, CB10 1HR, 01799 525 421
Gluttons, 2–3 Rose & Crown Walk, CB10 1JH, 01799 522892

Stamford, Lincolnshire

Tourist Information Centre, Stamford Arts Centre, 27 St Mary's Street, PE9 1PJ, 01780 755611

WHERE TO STAY
The George Hotel of Stamford, High Street, St. Martin's, PE9 2LB, 01780 750750

The Crown, 6 All Saints' Place, PE9 2AG, 01780 763136
The Garden House Hotel, 42 High Street, St. Martin's, PE9 2LP, 01780 763359
Birch House, 4 Lonsdale Road, PE9 2RW, 01780 754876
WHERE TO EAT
Oakhouse, 11 All Saints' Place, PE9 2AR, 01780 756565
The Meadows Restaurant, 1–2 Castle Street, PE9 2RA, 01780 762739
The Candlesticks Restaurant, 1 Church Lane, PE9 2JU, 01780 764033

Swaffham, Norfolk

Tourist Information Centre, Market Place, Swaffham, PE37 7AB , 01760 722255

WHERE TO STAY
The George Hotel, Station Street, PE37 7LJ, 01760 721238
The Horse & Groom, 40 Lynn Street, PE37 7AX, 01760 721567
Stratton Hotel, 4 Ash Close, PE37 7NH, 01760 723845
Lydney House Hotel, Norwich Road, PE37 7QS, 01760 723355
WHERE TO EAT
Romford House, 5 London Street, PE37 7DD, 01760 722552

Wisbech, Cambridgeshire

Tourist Information Centre, 2–3 Bridge Street, PE13 1EW, 01945 583263

WHERE TO STAY
The White Lion Hotel, 5 South Brink, PE13 1JD, 01945 589851
Phoenix Hotel, 5 North Brink, PE13 1JR, 01945 474559
Angel Inn, 45 Alexandra Road, PE13 1HT, 01945 589794
Algethi Guest House, 136 Lynn Road, PE13 3DP, 01945 582278
WHERE TO EAT
Rose and Crown Hotel, Market Place, PE13 1DG, 01945 589800
Red Lion, 32 North Brink, PE13 1JX, 01945 582022

The Southern Counties

Farnham, Surrey

Tourist Information Centre, Council Offices, South Street, GU9 7RN, 01252 715109

WHERE TO STAY
The Bush Hotel, The Borough, GU9 7NN, 0870 400 8225/ 01252 715237
Bishop's Table Best Western, 27 West Street, GU9 7DR, 01252 710222
Farnham Park Hotel, Lower Hale, GU9 9RP, 01252 728603
1 Park Row, 1 Park Row, GU9 7JH, 07880 541120
WHERE TO EAT
The Hop Blossom, 50 Long Garden Walk, GU9 7HX, 01252 710770
Vienna Stuberl, 112 West Street, GU9 7HH, 01252 722978
The Colony Peking Cuisine, 68 Castle Street, GU9 7LN, 01252 725108

Faversham, Kent

Tourist Information Centre, 10–13 Preston Street, ME13 8NS, 01795 534542

WHERE TO STAY
Read's Restaurant, Macknade Manor, Canterbury Road, ME13 8XE, 01795 535344
The Sun Inn, West Street, ME13 7JE, 01795 535098
Tanners Cottage, 37 Tanners St, ME13 7JP, 01795 536698
March Cottage Bed & Breakfast, 5 Preston Avenue, ME13 8NH, 01795 536514

WHERE TO EAT
Read's Restaurant, Macknade Manor, Canterbury Road, ME13 8XE, 01795 535344
The Dove, Plum Pudding Lane, Dargate, ME13 9HB, 01227 751360

Hastings, East Sussex

Tourist Information Centre, Queen Square, TN34 1TZ, 01424 781111

WHERE TO STAY
Chatsworth Hotel, Carlisle Parade, TN34 1JG, 01424 720188
Cinque Ports Hotel, Bohemia Road, TN34 1ET, 01424 439222
Sinclair House Bed & Breakfast, 6 Baldslow Road, TN34 2EZ, 01424 420347
Holyers, 1 Hill Street, Old Town, TN34 3HU, 01424 430014
The Astral Lodge, 4 Carlisle Parade, TN34 1JG, 01424 445599
WHERE TO EAT
Hastings Arms, 2 George Street, TN34 3EG, 01424 722208
Gannets Bistro, 45 High Street, TN34 3EN, 01424 439678
Mermaid Café, 2 Rock-a-Nore Road, TN34 3DW, 01424 438100

Lymington, Hampshire

Tourist Information Centre, New Street, SO41 9BH, 01590 689000

WHERE TO STAY
Stanwell House, 14–15 High Street, SO41 9AA, 01590 677123
Elmers Court, South Baddesley Road, SO41 5ZB, 01590 676011
Dolphins Bed & Breakfast, 6 Emsworth Road, 01590 676108
Britannia House, Mill Lane, 01590 672091
WHERE TO EAT
Egan's Restaurant, Gosport Street, SO41 9BE, 01590 676165
Ship Inn, Quay Road, SO41 3AY, 01590 672903

Petworth, West Sussex

Tourist Information Centre, Petworth Area Office, The Old Bakery, Golden Square, GU28 0AP, 01798 343523

WHERE TO STAY
The Stonemason's Inn, North Street, GU28 9NL, 01798 342510
The Angel Inn, Angel Street, GU28 0BG, 01798 342153
Old Railway Station, Station Road, GU28 0JF, 01798 342346
WHERE TO EAT
The Cricketers, Duncton Green, GU28 0LB, 01798 342473
Soanes Restaurant, Grove Lane, GU28 0HY, 01798 343659

The Western Counties

Bradford-on-Avon, Wiltshire

Tourist Information Centre, 50 St. Margaret's Street, BA15 1DE, 01225 865797

WHERE TO STAY
Georgian Lodge, 25 Bridge Street, BA15 1BY, 01225 862268
The Swan Hotel, Church Street, BA15 1LN, 01225 868686
Bradford Old Windmill, 4 Masons Lane, BA15 1QN, 01225 866842
Tory, 29 Tory, BA15 1NN, 01225 864935
WHERE TO EAT
Le Mangetout, Knees Corner, Silver Street, BA15 1JR, 01225 863111
Bunch of Grapes, 14 Silver Street, BA15 1JY, 01225 863877
The Bridge Tea Rooms, 24a Bridge Street, BA15 1BY 01225 865537

Glastonbury, Somerset

Tourist Information Centre, The Tribunal, 9 High Street, BA6 9DP, 01458 832954

WHERE TO STAY

Number Three, 3 Magdalene Street, BA6 9EW, 01458 832129
George and Pilgrims, 1 High Street, BA6 9DP, 01458 831146
Apple Tree House, 27 Bere Lane, BA6 8BD, 01458 830803
Shambhala Healing Retreat, Coursing Batch, BA6 8BH, 01458 831797
The Who'd A Thought It Inn, 17 Northload Street, BA6 9JJ, 01458 834460

WHERE TO EAT

The Market House Inn, 12-14 Magdalene Street, BA6 9EH, 01458 832220
Blue Note Café, 4 High Street, BA6 9DU, 01458 832907
Abbey Tea Rooms, 16 Magdalene Street, BA6 9EH, 01458 832852

Shaftesbury, Dorset

Tourist Information Centre, 8 Bell Street, SP7 8AE, 01747 85351

WHERE TO STAY

Grosvenor Hotel, The Commons, SP7 8JA, 01747 852282
The Knoll, Bleke Street, SP7 8AH, 01747 855243
Milland House, Breach Lane, SP7 8LF, 01747 852742
The Retreat, 47 Bell Street, SP7 8AE, 01747 850372

WHERE TO EAT

La Fleur de Lys, Bleke Street, SP7 8AW, 01747 853717
The Wayfarers, Sherborne Causeway, SP7 9PX, 01747 852821
The Salt Cellar, 2–3 Gold Hill, SP7 8LY, 01747 851838

St. Ives, Cornwall

Tourist Information Centre, The Guildhall, Street-an-Pol, TR26 2DS, 01736 796297

WHERE TO STAY

Blue Hayes Hotel, Trelyon Avenue, TR26 2AD, 01736 797129
Western Hotel, Royal Square, TR26 2ND, 01736 795277
Chy Lelan Guest House, Bunkers Hill, TR26 1LJ, 01736 797560
White Waves, 4 Sea View Terrace, TR26 2DH, 01736 797374
Nancherrow Cottage, 7 Fish Street, TR26 1LT, 01736 798496

WHERE TO EAT

Alba, Old Lifeboat House, Wharf Road, TR26 1LF, 01736 797222
Blue Fish Restaurant, Norway Lane, TR26 1LZ, 01736 794204
Alfresco Café Bar, The Wharf, TR26 1LF, 01736 793737
The Pickled Fish, 3 Chapel Street, TR26 2LR, 01736 795100

Totnes, Devonshire

Tourist Information Centre, The Town Mill, Coronation Road, TQ9 5DF, 01803 863168

WHERE TO STAY

Royal Seven Stars, The Plains, TQ9 5DD, 01803 862125
The Steam Packet Inn, St Peter's Quay, TQ9 5EW, 01803 863880
1 The Mount, Totnes Downhill, TQ9 5ES, 01803 847679
The Old Forge at Totnes, Seymour Place, TQ9 5AY, 01803 862174
Corner Cottage, 12 Cistern Street, TQ9 5SP, 01803 86434

WHERE TO EAT

Effings, 50 Fore Street, TQ9 5RP, 01803 863435
Will's Restaurant, 3 The Plains, TQ9 5DR, 01803 865192
The Willow Vegetarian Restaurant, 87 High Street, TQ9 5PB, 01803 862605

Further Reading

BETJEMAN, John, *English Cities and Small Towns*, London, 1943
BRIGGS, Asa, *A Social History of England*, London, 1983
COBBETT, William, *Rural Rides*; edited with an introduction by George Woodcock, Harmondsworth, 1967
PEVSNER, Nikolaus, *The Buildings of England,* Harmondsworth, various dates
PRIESTLEY, J.B., *English Journey*, London, 1934
QUINEY, Anthony, *The English Country Town*, London, 1987
JENKINS, Simon, *England's Thousand Best Churches*, London, 1999